THE LITTLE BOOK OF

Trauma Healing

Minnesota
Peacebuilding
Leadership
Institute

www.mnpeace.org

Published titles include:

The Little Book of Restorative Justice: Revised & Updated,
by Howard Zehr

The Little Book of Conflict Transformation, by John Paul Lederach

The Little Book of Family Group Conferences, New-Zealand Style,
by Allan MacRae and Howard Zehr

The Little Book of Strategic Peacebuilding, by Lisa Schirch

The Little Book of Strategic Negotiation,
by Jayne Seminare Docherty

The Little Book of Circle Processes, by Kay Pranis

The Little Book of Contemplative Photography, by Howard Zehr

The Little Book of Restorative Discipline for Schools,
by Lorraine Stutzman Amstutz and Judy H. Mullet

The Little Book of Trauma Healing, by Carolyn E. Yoder

The Little Book of Biblical Justice, by Chris Marshall

The Little Book of Restorative Justice for People in Prison,
by Barb Toews

The Little Book of Cool Tools for Hot Topics,
by Ron Kraybill and Evelyn Wright

El Pequeño Libro de Justicia Restaurativa, by Howard Zehr

The Little Book of Dialogue for Difficult Subjects,
by Lisa Schirch and David Campt

The Little Book of Victim Offender Conferencing,
by Lorraine Stutzman Amstutz

The Little Book of Restorative Justice for Colleges and Universities,
by David R. Karp

The Little Book of Restorative Justice for Sexual Abuse, by Judah
Oudshoorn with Michelle Jackett and Lorraine Stutzman Amstutz

The Big Book of Restorative Justice: Four Classic Justice &
Peacebuilding Books in One Volume, by Howard Zehr, Lorraine
Stutzman Amstutz, Allan MacRae, and Kay Pranis

The Little Book of Transformative Community Conferencing,
by David Anderson Hooker

The Little Book of Restorative Justice in Education,
by Katherine Evans and Dorothy Vaandering

The Little Book of Restorative Justice for Older Adults,
by Julie Friesen and Wendy Meek

The Little Books of Justice & Peacebuilding present, in highly accessible
form, key concepts and practices from the fields of restorative justice,
conflict transformation, and peacebuilding. Written by leaders in these fields,
they are designed for practitioners, students, and anyone interested in justice,
peace, and conflict resolution.

The Little Books of Justice & Peacebuilding series is a cooperative effort
between the Center for Justice and Peacebuilding of Eastern Mennonite
University and publisher Good Books.

THE LITTLE BOOK OF

Trauma Healing

Revised & Updated

*When Violence Strikes and
Community Security Is Threatened*

CAROLYN E. YODER

New York, New York

Good Books books may be purchased in bulk at special discounts for sales promotion, corporate gifts, fund-raising, or educational purposes. Special editions can also be created to specifications. For details, contact the Special Sales Department, Good Books, 207 West 36th Street, 11th Floor, New York, NY 10018 or info@skyhorsepublishing.com.

Good Books is an imprint of Skyhorse Publishing, Inc.®, a Delaware corporation.

Visit our website at www.goodbooks.com

10 9 8 7 6 5 4 3 2 1

Library of Congress Cataloging-in-Publication Data is available on file.

Print ISBN: 978-1-68099-603-6
eBook ISBN: 978-1-68099-636-4

Printed in the United States of America

For Doreen Ruto Jemutai

After the 1998 bombing of the United States Embassy in Nairobi, Kenya, left Doreen a widow with two young sons, she embarked on a journey that included the Center for Justice and Peacebuilding at Eastern Mennonite University where she studied trauma, resilience, restorative justice, and peacebuilding on a Fulbright Student Scholarship.

Turning her pain and loss into a gift for others facing violence, she returned to her homeland Kenya where she founded Daima Initiatives for Peace and Development. Among her many accomplishments, she brought STAR (Strategies for Trauma Awareness and Resilience) trainings to hundreds, perhaps thousands in Kenya, Rwanda, the Somali region, and South Sudan.

Doreen's sudden death on January 21, 2016, leaves a void in the STAR community and in the hearts of all who loved her. Rest in Peace, Doreen.

Table of Contents

Acknowledgments

This *Little Book* is possible because many people offered a piece of themselves to create a work greater than the sum of its parts. I am grateful to the following, without whom the STAR program and this book would not exist:

- Church World Service and Rick Augsburger, CWS Director of Disaster Response, for the mandate and generous funding to create a trauma program after 9/11
- The Center for Justice and Peacebuilding (CJP) faculty and staff at Eastern Mennonite University. Your collaboration made this innovative paradigm and multidisciplinary training program possible. Thank you, Jayne Docherty, PhD (human security and peacebuilding), Barry Hart, PhD (trauma healing and peacebuilding), Vernon Jantzi, PhD (peacebuilding and Department Chair), Janice Jenner (CJP Practice Institute Director), Ron Kraybill, PhD (peacebuilding), Lisa Schirch, PhD (human security and peacebuilding), Nancy Good, PhD (trauma healing), and Howard Zehr, PhD (restorative justice). Others who contributed to the creation of STAR are Elaine Zook Barge, Vesna Hart, Amy Potter Czajkowski, Amela Puljek-Shank, the STAR

NYC office Codirectors Brenda Boyd Bell, PhD, and Ruth Wenger Yoder, and the thousands of STAR training participants from around the world whose feedback continues to leave an indelible mark on the content.

- The Center for Strategic and International Studies in Washington, DC (David Steele, Olga Botcharova, Barry Hart, Gerald Shenk), for their Seven Steps toward Revenge and Seven Steps toward Forgiveness models.
- STAR staff support services: Sharon Forret, Hannah Kelly, Shanti Martin Brown, Marsha Thomas, Kathy Smith, Robert Yutzy.
- Manuscript reviewers: Kristin Rothwell DeMello, Rick Yoder.
- Content consultants: Elaine Zook Barge, Jayne Docherty, Joy Kreider, Donna Minter, Kathryn Mansfield, Howard Zehr.
- For the gift of your personal stories: Lam Cosmas and "Anna Kelly."
- The Little Books series editor, Howard Zehr; Good Books and Skyhorse Publishing.
- Copy editors Cari Dubiel and Jim Clemens.
- Content editor Marian Sandmier of The Gentle Pen, whose fine-tuning was as gracious as the name suggests.

Most of all, thank you to my husband and best friend, Rick. For more than four decades your love and contagious zest for life have both enlivened and been a grounding support for this journey.

—Carolyn Yoder, Harrisonburg, Virginia

Preface:
STAR Beginnings

"You'll retraumatize people if you talk
about that peace stuff."
—Warning from a New York City focus group,
raw from 9/11,
reviewing the STAR curriculum prior
to the first training

The core framework of this book comes from Strategies for Trauma Awareness and Resilience (STAR), a justice and conflict informed approach to addressing trauma, which emerged from the attacks of 9/11. As the rubble of the twin towers smoldered, Church World Service in NYC recognized the need for a response that went beyond material aid. They provided funding to the Center for Justice and Peacebuilding (CJP) at Eastern Mennonite University to develop and implement a training program for civil society leaders around the world whose communities were impacted by the attacks and the global aftermath they sensed would ensue.

Hired to direct this unformed initiative, and fresh from working with trauma as a psychotherapist in the Middle East and Africa, I couldn't have landed in a better place. I had questions about the adequacy of a Western psychological paradigm in community trauma and in settings outside (and sometimes even inside) the Western world. I believed the emerging brain science, energy psychology, and body-based trauma approaches were relevant to the conflict and violence I'd witnessed. I sensed that finding nonviolent ways to work for security and justice was as much a trauma intervention as deep breathing and cognitive reframing. So was learning conflict transformation skills to address structural and relational issues at the root of violence and trauma. My thinking meshed with and complemented the experience and expertise of the CJP faculty and staff.

Together, we outlined the first version of a weeklong training. We couldn't find a theoretical framework to fit what we envisioned so we created our own by expanding and adapting a model that the Center for Strategic and International Studies in

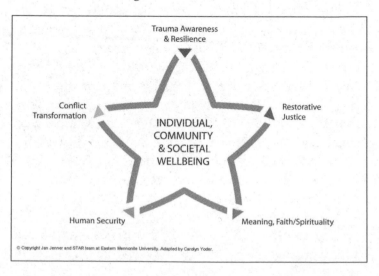

Trauma Awareness & Resilience

Conflict Transformation

Restorative Justice

INDIVIDUAL, COMMUNITY & SOCIETAL WELLBEING

Human Security

Meaning, Faith/Spirituality

© Copyright Jan Jenner and STAR team at Eastern Mennonite University. Adapted by Carolyn Yoder.

Washington, DC, developed in post-conflict work in the former Yugoslavia.[1] Through the ups and downs of the collaborative process of creating an innovative, evidence-supported paradigm and training program, belief in the mission of STAR and the common good triumphed over individualism. None of us could have created this program by ourselves.

The STAR approach integrates concepts from traditionally separate fields of study and practice: interpersonal neurobiology, psychology, human security, restorative justice, conflict transformation, and faith/spirituality. These disciplines we drew from are part of the field of peacebuilding. Human security expert Lisa Schirch defines peacebuilding as work "to prevent, reduce, transform, and help people recover from violence in all forms, even structural violence that has not yet led to civil unrest."[2]

Traumagenic

Likely to cause trauma for the majority of those who are targeted, for perpetrators, and for witnesses.

—Hooker and Czajkowski, 2013

Obviously, the STAR approach goes beyond the traditional medical model of trauma which has largely focused on psychological understandings and mental health professionals treating individuals. We need psychiatrists and psychologists. But given the sheer number of people impacted by traumagenic[3] systems and events, there is also an urgent need for trauma work to move out of quiet consulting rooms and into schools, public libraries, parks, mosques, temples, churches, gyms, and town halls. There is an urgent need for the general public to be trauma informed: educators, market vendors, humanitarian and development workers, clergy, factory workers, medical personnel, parents, government workers, welders, legislators, janitors, journalists, mayors, and soldiers. There is a need to expand our understanding of trauma treatment and interventions.

To this end, most participants in the STAR week-long trainings are not mental health professionals but people who rub shoulders daily with trauma-impacted individuals or groups in their families, organizations, or society. Often, they've experienced trauma themselves. The emphasis is on working in their communities, but many of the understandings, skills, and tools are readily adaptable and applicable to individuals. Indeed, the STAR approach is based on the importance of connecting personal understanding and healing from trauma with societal and structural responses that address the causes and consequences of conflict and violence.

STAR began as a two-year project for a post-9/11 world in a predominately white peace and justice-oriented Mennonite university in the United States and has been shaped over the years by thousands of training participants from around the world. The initial proposal for STAR included funding to bring at least four participants from violence affected countries to attend the monthly week-long workshops. They and participants from marginalized communities in the United Stated helped put the 9/11 events in perspective, raising hard questions about living under traumagenic systems and conditions day after day, year after year, and decade after decade.

Consequently, people across a wide intersectional spectrum of settings and identities have found the evidence-supported STAR framework can be meaningfully applied to their experience: historical harms,[4] natural disasters,[5] sexual and domestic violence,[6] racial injustice healing initiatives,[7] post-conflict settings,[8] and more.

And despite our initial trepidation that we might retraumatize our training participants by talking about nonviolent responses to threat and harm, the opposite happened. Responses in the training sessions and post-training evaluations showed that expanding beyond traditional psychological trauma interventions to include processes and tools of justice, security, and conflict transformation struck a deep chord in many. In fact, "that peace stuff" was the most requested follow-up training topic by participants from New York City in the early years of the program.

This book covers the STAR core concepts. But the experiential application exercises done in the trainings that can be used back home and the life-changing ah-ha moments can't be conveyed in a book. Join us in-person for that! www.emu.edu/star

This is not a book of definitive answers and solutions. Rather, it is the framework, theories, and questions that emerged from using STAR in hundreds of trainings on six continents. Applying trauma and resilience principles and practices to our communities is a paradigm shift. No one book can cover all the implications: issues of ongoing trauma, abuse, and harm are noted, but many of the examples will focus on trauma caused by violence and sudden catastrophes. And a warning: since the topic is trauma, some of the examples may be triggering.

As you read, think about applications to your own life, your community, organization, people, and nation. Addressing trauma and breaking/preventing cycles of violence in turbulent times is complex. But change begins as we listen, observe, wonder, imagine, pray, experiment, and then share what we're learning. This book comes to you in that spirit. Let's begin!

1.
Introduction

"Hurt people hurt people." (origin unknown)

"Transformed people transform people."
—*Richard Rohr, OFM*

We live in challenging times. Measured by the number of people affected by violence, the last century may have been the most brutal in human history.[1] Now, in the new millennium, conflict, division, inequality, nationalism, and terrorism continue to impact us and our planet. Hovering over all, climate crisis is a threatening omnipresent cloud, alarmingly visible to some and roundly ignored or denied by others.

As our global family struggles to find answers, little is said about the links between trauma and violence. Politicians, negotiators, peacebuilders, and the general public may be more aware of trauma than they were a decade ago, but many still think of it as something psychological that resilient people get over quickly. Mental health initiatives may be funded for short periods after earthquakes or school shootings, but they often are viewed as having little to do with

1

realpolitik and reducing violence. Yet trauma and violence are integrally linked: Hurt people hurt people. Violence often leads to trauma, and in turn, unhealed trauma can lead to further division, violence, and loss of security.

> Trauma and violence are integrally linked.

Trauma expert Bessel van der Kolk says trauma is arguably the number one public health issue in the United States, the greatest threat to national well-being.[2] Trauma affects our very physiology, including our ability to engage in full and integrated brain processing. John Gottman, a researcher on predictors of marital relationship success or failure, has found that when our pulse rate increases as little as ten beats above our usual baseline, the rational part of our brain begins slipping out of gear.[3] We then begin talking and behaving from the lower part of our brain, home of our automatic survival instincts.

If this physiological change occurs over who cleans up the kitchen, what happens in the body/brain when national leaders are challenged to respond to structural violence or terrorist attacks? What happens when people subjected to years of injustice and dignity violations are insulted once again? When groups are highly polarized? When negotiators sit around a bargaining table discussing disputed territory?

Being trauma-informed—having an awareness of what trauma is and how it impacts us physiologically, emotionally, mentally, and spiritually—is an important factor in helping to explain a wide range of phenomena such as feelings of insecurity, loss of cultural identity, racism, polarization, climate inaction, and violence overall.

But understanding trauma holds the potential to do more than explain. When we go a step beyond awareness and learn to address current, transgenerational, and historical trauma, we tap into the potential to heal wounds and transform individuals, communities, and societies. We enhance our ability to think creatively, respond compassionately, and work collaboratively for the good of all. We connect to our innate resilience.

Indeed, disruptive, disorienting times have the potential to awaken the human spirit, even the global family, to a new level of consciousness. It doesn't happen automatically, however. It requires that we learn to use our bodies in new ways, acknowledge our own history and that of "the other," search honestly for root causes, and shift our thinking from national security to human security.

At its core, addressing trauma is bio-psycho-social-spiritual work of the deepest sort, calling forth nothing less than our noblest ideals and the faith, hope, love, and resilience of the human spirit.

These are bold assertions. But they are the big ideas of this *Little Book*.

To access the study guide for this book, go to skyhorsepublishing.com/go/9781680996036. Click on "More Details" and then scroll down to "Links."

2.
Definition,
Sources, and Types
of Trauma

The trauma vignettes in this chapter and throughout the book may be difficult for some readers.

- *The tranquility of Lam Cosmas's youth in Northern Uganda was shattered in 1986 when rebels began raiding cattle and attacking unarmed civilians. Over the next several years, villages were attacked, crops burned, and men and women killed. Nighttime raids took boys as young as seven to be child soldiers and girls as young as nine to be "wives" to the rebels. The terrified villagers moved to urban centers in droves, where they lived in crowded camps for internally displaced persons that lacked the most basic amenities.*[1]
- *In the aftermath of Hurricane Maria, which devastated the island of Puerto Rico in 2017, Juan Reus's father-in-law died in a nursing home that*

had lost power. Another friend died of a bacterial infection spread through floodwaters, and a third burned to death in a gas explosion. A combination of politics, poor preplanning, disorganized after-response, and the impact of rising temperatures from climate change combined to make the natural disaster catastrophic. "The hurricane," Reus says, "hit us like an atomic bomb."[2]

- *Tamir Rice, a twelve-year-old African American boy, was killed by police in a Cleveland park in 2014 as he played with a toy gun. Data from 2015 to mid-2018 show African Americans are 54 percent more likely to be unarmed when killed by police compared to whites and that they are victims of the lethal use of force by police at nearly twice their rate in the general population.[3]*

- *Leila Begum's husband and two sons were killed when the Myanmar military attacked her Rohingya village. She and her two daughters fled, then trekked for six days to reach a refugee camp in Bangladesh. "I cried the whole way," she says. She worries how she will feed and educate her daughters.[4]*

- *Linda Maloney, a member of the Mi'kmaq First Nation of Nova Scotia, is a survivor of the Canadian residential school system for Aboriginal children. She recalls her older sisters not being allowed to comfort her when she was lonely, and the strappings and indignity of having one's head shaved for speaking Mi'kmaq. "They were trying to assimilate us," she says. "They just wanted to get rid of the Indians."[5]*

- *On September 11, 2001, Anna Kelly (name has been changed) was at work in her California office when a neighbor called and told her to turn on the TV. As she watched the World Trade Towers go up in flames and then collapse, Anna slumped from her chair to the floor. She knew that her brother, a firefighter in southern Manhattan, would be there.*

- *Justina Masika Bihama grew up in Goma, Democratic Republic of Congo, which has been called "the rape capital of the world." She prefers to call it the "world capital of sisterhood and solidarity." "We have few resources, but we have an enormous amount of know-how," she says. She has received death threats for her stance and her home and office have been raided.[6]*

In casual conversation, the word "trauma" is used to describe reactions to anything from a stressful day to a brutal murder. Trauma, from *traumat,* a Greek word meaning *wound,* refers to an individual's or group's reactions and response—physical, emotional, cognitive, spiritual, and relational—to terrible events like those described above. These events differ in intensity and/or duration from ordinary stress and overwhelm us.

Whether or not a situation is overwhelming cannot be determined by looking only at the event. What is merely stressful for one individual or community may be traumatic for another, depending on a combination of factors which include the quality of social support available, knowledge of how to deal with trauma, age, previous trauma history, genetic makeup, and the meaning a person or society gives to what happened.[7]

Traumagenic events:

Often involve threats to life or our bodies.
Produce terror and feelings of helplessness.
Overwhelm an individual or group's ability to cope or respond to the threat.
Lead to a sense of loss of control.
Challenge a person's or group's sense that life is meaningful and orderly.

To distinguish an event from people's response to it, some prefer the word *traumagenic*,[8] which means capable of causing trauma, much like a carcinogenic substance has the potential to cause cancer but may not. Individuals or groups may or may not experience trauma in response to a terrible event. *Consequently, a traumatic reaction needs to be treated as valid regardless of how the event that induced it appears to anyone else.*

Traumagenic events occur in social systems, and our responses are significantly influenced by interactions between the individual and the surrounding society.[9] Kadzu, for example, has AIDS, which she contracted from her husband, who died a year ago. She and her two sons live with her elderly widowed mother and are financially dependent on their economically stretched extended family. Kadzu's situation is impacted by the attitude of her family, community, and nation toward AIDS and the resources available for prevention and treatment, as well as the intellectual property rights, drug prices, and patents of multinational pharmaceutical companies. The latter, in turn, are affected by international trade agreements. Kadzu's resilience, her capacity to maintain or regain a sense of balance and wellness in the face of adversity, is not only about her individual traits. The ability to be resilient is also embedded in our social web.

Ongoing and structurally induced trauma

Not all trauma results from a single, dramatic, rarely experienced event such as a tornado, a serious accident, or even the death of Anna's brother in the World Trade Center. Trauma can be the result of living under abusive or unsafe conditions that are long-term, with no known endpoint. This is the case with the ongoing civil war in Lam's story or the struggle to survive in Leila's. The constant specter of death or injury where populations live in conflict zones, in poverty-stricken or dangerous neighborhoods, under occupation, or in fear of terrorism, may be routine, but they are traumagenic.

Another cause of trauma is the ongoing structural violence of the economic, legal, and social systems which result in people's basic human needs for food, shelter, education, health care, and justice not being met. Often, these structurally induced traumas go unnoticed by those more privileged until an event such as a natural disaster or the surveillance video of Tamir Rice's death graphically exposes injustices that have festered for years.

The trauma literature provides various descriptors for the experience or consequences of living with ongoing trauma: cumulative trauma, continuous trauma, chronic trauma, complex trauma, and sequential, multiple, or plural traumas. Perhaps psychologist Martha Cabrera, who works on trauma recovery programs in communities in Nicaragua, describes it best when she says that after experiencing natural disasters and several decades of conflict, Nicaragua is "a multiply wounded, multiply traumatized, multiply mourning country."[10] The psychological, spiritual, social, economic, and political effects of these difficult conditions can be profound not only for individuals, but also for entire societies.

Collective, organizational, shared, and planetary trauma

When a traumatic event or series of events affects large numbers of people, we speak of societal, mass, or collective trauma. The traumagenic events may be experienced directly, but trauma can also occur from witnessing—or merely hearing about—horrific events. Whether direct or indirect, a traumagenic group experience can set off widespread fear, horror, helplessness, or anger, impacting an entire region or nation.

Organizational trauma is "a collective experience that overwhelms the organization's defensive and protective structures and leaves the entity temporarily vulnerable and helpless or permanently damaged."[11] The effects are systemic, and, if left unaddressed, weaken the organization, compromising its work and long-term health.

Shared trauma is when both helping professionals and their clients have experienced the same collective trauma.[12] Within a society, cultural subgroups may experience traumagenic events differently, depending on their proximity to the threat or the degree to which they identify with the victims of the events.

Climate crisis introduces an unprecedented collective challenge to all species on the planet. We have no experience with a threat of this type or magnitude. The normal trauma responses we discuss in the next chapter are evident in the responses of individuals, nations, and international bodies: fight (struggle/ preventive action), flight (denial/spiritualizing), and freeze/collapse (helplessness/inaction). Harvard psychology professor Daniel Gilbert believes we do so little about the climate crisis because our brains are attuned to respond strongly to four types of threats: Personal, Abrupt, Immoral, and Now (PAIN). Climate change rarely triggers any of these,[13] although personal impacts are increasing. What psychologists call eco-anxiety is on the rise.[14] In spite of our surface behaviors, some part of us is aware.

Historical trauma transferred through the generations

Native American Maria Yellow Horse Brave Heart, PhD, known for her critical work exploring and describing indigenous collective trauma, defines historical trauma as the "cumulative emotional and psychological wounding over the life span and across generations emanating from massive group trauma."[15,16] Examples include enslavement, colonialism, and persecution or genocide of an ethnic, national, or religious group. The "event" or institution is in the past, but the lingering effects are seen in the attitudes and behaviors of succeeding generations. Often a "conspiracy of silence" surrounds events for which grieving and mourning have never taken place.[17]

The transgenerational transmission of trauma can occur even when the next generation is not told the trauma story or knows it only in broad outline. Studies in the field of epigenetics indicate that past and future generations are connected in ways we never imagined possible—through genomic imprinting. This means that more than DNA is transmitted from one generation to another: our genes carry a memory of the experience of our ancestors and transmit that information from one generation to the next.[18,19,20,21] This emotional imprinting has implications for our health, including our own and our descendants' ability to be resilient in the face of trauma. It raises the question as to whether further epigenetic study will find that *addressing trauma* reverses the negative impacts on us and future generations.

> Our genes carry a memory of the experience of our ancestors.

Perpetration-induced trauma

Another source of trauma is rarely discussed: being an active participant in causing harm to others, whether by accident, in the line of duty, or outside the law, as in organized crime or gang activity. Research by psychologist Rachael MacNair suggests that the traumatic effects of harming others, intentionally or unintentionally, can be as severe or even *more* severe than the suffering that victims and survivors experience.[22] The issues MacNair raises have significant implications for communities and nations. What are the psychological and spiritual implications for groups or nations that bear responsibility for genocide, torching villages of minority ethnic groups, mass incarceration, separating asylum-seekers from their children, gender discrimination, rape as a weapon, military occupation, suicide bombings, state-supported assassinations, or preemptive wars? The concept of moral injury, the damage done when one violates his/her own values,

11

has been mostly applied to individuals.[23,24] It also is relevant to the collective.[25]

Secondary trauma

Secondary trauma refers to the effects experienced by those interacting with trauma survivors: family members living with a traumatized person, first responders, medical and mental health professionals, peacebuilders, humanitarian workers, and development specialists who work with trauma-exposed populations. For example, even though reporters who covered the testimonies of victims in South Africa's Truth and Reconciliation Commission were given background briefings on how to identify and avoid becoming personally traumatized, many reported post-traumatic stress reactions from listening to the testimony of victims of apartheid. The effects of secondary trauma (nightmares, flashbacks, headaches, insomnia) are like those experienced by victims and survivors themselves. Organizations that work with trauma-impacted populations have a responsibility to recognize when shared or secondary trauma put their staff at risk.

A word about terrorism

Terrorism is a major concern in our world that fits into several of the above categories. The term terrorism is often used loosely, so it is important to state the understanding used in this book. According to Cunningham,[26] terrorism has four key elements:

1. It involves an act in which violence or force is used or threatened.
2. It is primarily a political act.
3. It is intended to cause fear or terror.

4. Its goal is to achieve physiological effects and reactions.

Objectivity breaks down in discussions of terrorism precisely because terrorist acts engender an emotionally charged trauma response in the victims, their communities, and in those who sympathize with them. Radical groups as well as nation states can perpetrate acts of terror.

In summary

Traumatic events and situations engender feelings of powerlessness and overwhelm our usual ability to effectively cope with threats. The following can be the source of trauma:

- Abuse or assault: physical, emotional, spiritual, sexual (rape)
- Accidents and the resulting injury to self, or the injury or death caused to others[27]
- Betrayal
- Causing harm or death to others deliberately— for example, through criminal acts (torture, abuse, abuse of power, or terrorism, including state-sponsored or state-sanctioned terrorism), or in the line of duty (e.g. by law enforcement, executioners, or military personnel)
- Dignity violations that diminish and humiliate, such as microaggressions,[28] living under occupation, or being enslaved, abused, or neglected
- Homelessness, including the experience of being a refugee
- Human-caused disasters, such as chemical spills, dams that collapse, or a government agency's failure to respond or protect

- Identity-based discrimination based on factors such as religion, tribe, gender, sexual orientation, physical ability, etc.
- Mass violence: assault, massacres, genocide, war
- Medical and dental procedures, including surgeries, life-threatening illnesses, and difficult births
- Natural disasters, such as hurricanes, earthquakes, tornados, tsunamis
- Poverty, class discrimination
- Pandemics and epidemics such as AIDS, Ebola, and bioterrorism
- Racism, colorism[29]
- Structural violence, in which social structures, policies, or institutions deprive people of their land, culture, dignity, rights, or ability to meet basic needs
- Sudden loss of loved ones, status, identity, possessions, home, territory
- Threat to the social order through sudden changing of the rules, expectations, or norms; nationalism, hyper-partisanship
- Threat to our planet from the economic, political, and environmental impact of global climate collapse
- Trafficking, torture
- Violating our own values, ethics, or code of conduct resulting in harm to others
- Witnessing death or injury
- Working directly with victims and survivors

In summary, there are numerous sources and types of trauma. We turn now to the way we as individuals and societies are affected by traumagenic events, and common, normal responses.

3.
The Trauma Experience:
STAR Model Part I

L am Cosmas of Uganda remembers the date clearly: October 3.

I lived in Gulu, and I boarded a bus that morning to travel to the capital, Kampala. I was sitting near the center of the bus, and I got uneasy when we came to a spot about 16 kilometers from town because rebels had attacked a truck there not long ago. Then, through the window, I saw people in military fatigues squatting beside the road with their guns pointed. I was so afraid. I screamed at the driver, "Don't stop, don't stop." I heard bullets and the screams of the other passengers. I couldn't keep from shouting, "Don't stop! Don't stop!"

The driver revved the engine and sped down the road. I just remember some things: blood everywhere, people screaming, the face of a man hit in

*the jaw, a man whose legs were shot up. I was so
scared I didn't know if I was hurt or not. And the
children! Some of them were under the seats. It was
odd. They did not cry out or make a sound.*

*The driver stopped when we got to the next town,
about 50 kilometers from the scene. I checked my
body—no injuries. Those hurt were taken to the hos-
pital. No one died, but the man with the leg wounds
had both legs amputated. We inspected the bus and
found bullet holes right above the tires. Thank God
they didn't get the tires. Then we noticed that the
driver's trousers were bloody: he had been shot. You
know, he had felt no pain.*

Lam's horrific experience during an 18-year period
of insurgency in his country illustrates the impact of
trauma even if people escape with no bullet wounds.
To track and understand the way trauma, violence,
and security are interrelated, we will use the stories
of Lam and Anna, whose brother died in the 9/11
attacks in New York City, along with the three-part
STAR model, Breaking Cycles of Violence and Building Resilience.[1] In this chapter, we look at Part I of
the model, Trauma Experience on page 17, which
depicts common, normal responses to traumatic
events. The numbers in parentheses throughout this
chapter refer to the numbers on the model. Note that
although the reactions in the cycle are numbered
sequentially, in life they do not happen one at a time
or in a neat, linear order except for physiological
changes (#1, #2).

Trauma affects us physiologically

To understand trauma, we need to begin not with the psychological, but with the physical body, specifically the nervous system, which includes the brain.

You may be tempted to skip this section. But if you want to effectively address trauma, interrupt cycles of violence, and promote resilience and well-being, you need a basic understanding of how the body reacts physically to safety and fear. Those reactions drive the dynamics and behaviors of individuals and groups all over the world.

> With our first breath, we embark on a biologically driven quest to feel safe in our bodies, in our environments, and in our relationships with others.
>
> —Deb Dana, PhD

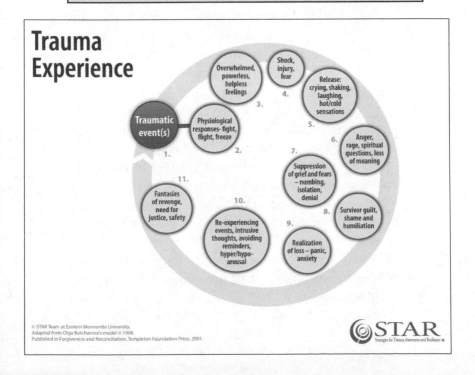

Trauma Experience

1. Traumatic event(s)
2. Physiological responses- fight, flight, freeze
3. Overwhelmed, powerless, helpless feelings
4. Shock, injury, fear
5. Release: crying, shaking, laughing, hot/cold sensations
6. Anger, rage, spiritual questions, loss of meaning
7. Suppression of grief and fears – numbing, isolation, denial
8. Survivor guilt, shame and humiliation
9. Realization of loss – panic, anxiety
10. Re-experiencing events, intrusive thoughts, avoiding reminders, hyper/hypo-arousal
11. Fantasies of revenge, need for justice, safety

STAR
Strategies for Trauma Awareness and Resilience ®

The most foundational fact is that regardless of our race, ethnicity, gender, nationality, class, or any other factor that can divide us, we all come into the world biologically wired to connect with each other. And we all are born with a need to feel safe.

Neuroscientist Stephen Porges's Polyvagal Theory describes three automatic nervous-system responses to safety or threat/fear that operate in us all: (1) the social engagement system (face-heart); (2) mobilization (fight/flight); and (3) immobilization (freeze/collapse).[2,3] Think of these three responses as three levels of a ladder, where without conscious thought, we move up or down all day long according to the biological response to how safe or threatened we feel in our bodies, our environments, and our relationships.[4] The closer to the top, the greater our feeling of safety

and the greater the degree of integrated brain functioning allowing us to respond to what is happening in multiple ways. The more we feel threat/fear, the lower we go on the ladder, and the more instinct-driven our behavior becomes as higher brain function goes increasingly "off-line." The principal communication "highway" of how safe or threatened we feel is the vagus nerve, the longest nerve in our body that wanders from the brain stem to the abdomen, connecting major organs along the way.

Brain and Vagus Nerves.
wellcomecollection.org.
Creative Commons License

Let's look more closely at each of these three nervous system responses, and how they relate to Lam and Anna's stories.

18

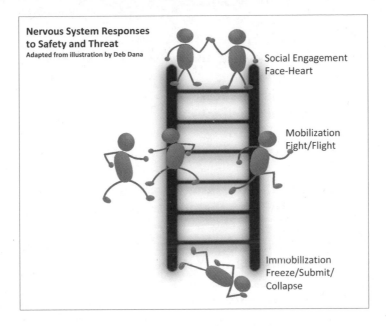

Nervous System Responses to Safety and Threat
Adapted from illustration by Deb Dana

Social Engagement
Face-Heart

Mobilization
Fight/Flight

Immobilization
Freeze/Submit/
Collapse

1. *The Social Engagement System (Face-Heart): The Highest Rung of the Ladder*
Under conditions of relative safety and manageable everyday challenges, we navigate the world and our relationships using what Porges calls our social engagement system.[5] Through a "face-heart" connection with each other, we use our tone of voice, facial expressions, posture, and the quality of our listening to send and receive cues of safety or threat.

Interpersonal neurobiologist Daniel Siegel paints a beautiful word picture of who we are when we are feeling safe in our environment, our bodies, and with each other. We are:

- able to keep our body coordinated and balanced;
- attuned to how others are feeling;

- emotionally balanced;
- capable of pausing and reflecting on options before responding;
- able to modulate fear;
- insightful and self-aware;
- able to feel empathy;
- capable of morality and acting for the common good;
- in touch with our intuition and nonrational ways of knowing that fuel wisdom.[6]

Imagine a marriage, an organization, a society, where everyone consistently functioned like this! Likely this is the state Lam was in as he chatted with other passengers at the start of the bus trip and what Anna experienced, safe in her office and absorbed in her work, that fateful September morning.

If we could peer inside Lam's and Anna's brains using modern imaging techniques, we would see the three major, interdependent parts of the brain working harmoniously together: the cerebral cortex (rational, thinking brain with a sense of past, present, and future time), the limbic system (emotional and memory center and home to the "first-alert alarm," the amygdala), and the brain stem (instinctual brain governing automatic functions such as breathing and heart rate and with no sense of time—everything is "NOW"). The limbic system and brain stem are sometimes grouped together and referred to as the lower brain.

A cluster of regions in the cerebral cortex, which Siegel calls "the middle prefrontal cortex," touch and connect the three major parts of the brain.[7] For ease of reference, I'll call those regions the "connecting

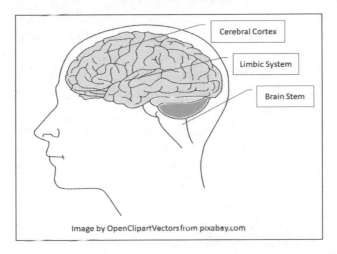

Image by OpenClipartVectors from pixabay.com

brain" throughout this book. Our amazing connecting brain links more than the three parts of the brain. By way of the vagus nerve, it also receives information about safety or threats in the environment from the organs and gut. It even reads signals from the brains of other people in our social world! No wonder when we feel safe and all three parts of the brain are working together, we connect positively with others, are courageous, calm, and brilliantly creative.

With such incredible wiring within us, why would we leave this virtual relationship-garden-of-Eden?

Lack of safety. And the resulting fear.

2. Mobilization (Fight/Flight): The Middle of the Ladder

Our brain/nervous system is constantly scanning for danger in and around our bodies and in our social interactions with others. Porges coined the word *neuroception* to describe this surveillance system that operates far below our conscious awareness and without the rational, thinking part of our brain.[8] It differs from perception, which comes from our senses and involves a degree of awareness.

When an earthquake shakes the ground beneath our feet or our group is humiliated by yet another dignity violation, neuroception alerts us to threat, and a lightning-quick assessment happens beneath our conscious awareness: Can we use our social connection and engagement skills, our first line of response, to deal with the threat? If yes, the information is routed to our rational brain, and the symphony of the connecting brain hums into action, modulating fear as we use the social engagement system—smiling, careful listening, creative problem-solving—to deal with the situation.

But if our neuroception says we are not safe, as when Lam saw the guns pointed at the bus, down the ladder we go and our second line of defense, mobilization (fight/flight), kicks in *before the thinking cerebral cortex is even consciously aware of the danger.* A cascade of stress chemicals and hormones releases instantly, resulting in a tornado-like rush of energy in the body. Heart rate, respiration, and metabolism surges. Blood rushes to the muscles to produce extra-strength energy. Any body function not needed for survival, such as digestion, shuts down. Capabilities we need to stay alive, such as eyesight, are instantly sharpened (#1, #2). All these are brainstem processes over which we have no conscious control.

Our lower brain, with its lightning-speed automatic responses, can literally save our lives, because waiting for the slower thinking, analyzing rational brain to figure out what to do could get us killed. But the fight/flight mobilization also disrupts the symphony-like functioning of the connecting brain as our social engagement system goes off-line to varying degrees, just as a storm knocks out power lines in parts of a city. The extent of impairment and duration of the disruption depends on the intensity of the traumagenic event, the quality of social support available, and the meaning given to what happened, among other factors.

The rush of energy in response to threat is what gives us the fuel for running away or fighting in the moment. If it's possible to physically fight or run away to deal with the threat, the tornado-like energy is utilized, and the body can calm down and return to a state of rest, completing a natural physiological cycle. We feel a sense of relief, exhilaration, and even triumph. Our social engagement system can come back online.

However, if the brain/nervous system senses that mobilization (fight/flight) isn't enough to ensure safety, or if running or fighting is impossible, as when Lam was trapped on the bus, the third line of defense automatically kicks in: immobilization.

3. *Immobilization (Freeze/Submit/Collapse): The Lowest Rung of the Ladder*
Immobilization, like mobilization (fight/flight), happens spontaneously and is not a conscious choice. The nervous system/lower brain is trying to help us survive. We become the proverbial "deer in the headlights," and the body shuts down physiologically (#2). We are unable to think, move, or talk. This is called freeze. In situations where we feel utterly powerless, such as a brutal sexual assault, the body may go into a state of collapse. We may faint or be so physically paralyzed that we look lifeless. We experience dissociation, a process of mental distancing from what is happening, that protects us from being overwhelmed

by the full emotional impact or the physical pain in the moment. People may experience a sense of detached calm. Time is distorted: events happen in slow motion or in an accelerated rush. Memories are not processed or stored in the usual way. They become fragmented, later producing graphic images on the one hand, and, paradoxically, an inability to recall on the other. The parts of the brain that control speech can shut down, giving rise to expressions such as "mute with terror" (#2, #3, #4).

Although the body is immobilized, stress chemicals and hormones continue to course through it. Freezing or collapsing while the tornado-like energy of fight-or-flight still has the nervous system in a state of hyperarousal is like pressing on the accelerator of a car while slamming on the brakes.

Mobilization/immobilization work best for "attacking-tiger" situations where a threat is present, then over, and the nervous system can recover and feel safe again. Situations of ongoing violence and threat keep us off-balance and going up and down the ladder. Twenty-first century mobilization/immobilization threats also come from being trapped in a meeting with a verbally abusive supervisor, buckled up in a cramped airline seat when turbulence is pressing our panic button, feeling helpless as harmful political actions are taken by governments, or we are attacked on social media. We may also feel immobilized by ongoing microaggressions, when caught between polarized groups, or as good jobs leave our region threatening our economic well-being.

These situations are registered as threat by our constantly-scanning neuroception surveillance system even if we can't run away or there's no one with a gun to our head we can fight. Yet the body keeps releasing stress chemicals and hormones, fueling energy that builds up inside us with nowhere to go. When not released, this constriction of energy is believed to be what produces many physiological trauma reactions such as flashbacks—*not* the actual event itself[9] (#10). It also provides the fuel for cycles of violence against ourselves and others, which we describe in the next chapter.

Lam continues:

Those of us who were not hurt continued on the three hours to Kampala. I don't remember much about the trip, except that near the end, one of the tires burst with a loud POP that sounded like a gunshot. Everyone screamed and crouched down in the seats. It was awful. Later, when I told my family what happened, I was trembling and perspiring. I had dreams about it for nearly three months, and I thought about it a lot, even though I tried not to. All these years later, I still feel fear when I pass the spot where it happened.

Brain researchers tell us that "neurons that fire together, wire together."[10] Neurons are specialized cells of the nervous system that carry messages through an electrochemical process. The more intense the experience is, the tighter they wire together. Later, sounds, sights, smells, or situations we experience that are similar to the original trauma can cause time to collapse and the trauma memory to rush back, vividly and unbidden. These are called intrusive memories (#10). We respond as if the event is happening *now* because the thinking brain with its sense of time is temporarily disrupted. Consequently, survivors seek to avoid these triggers, or reminders of what happened, so that they do not experience frighteningly vivid and intrusive flashbacks. They may withdraw from life, unable to be present in the here-and-now to themselves or their loved ones (#7).

For the passengers on Lam's bus, the emotion of fear became inextricably bound up with the sound of gunshots, the smell and sight of blood, the moans of the injured. Later, the sound of the tire blowing instantly triggered memories of the attack, sending him down the ladder and out of his social engagement system.

The shaking and sweating Lam experienced are natural physical trauma responses, the result of the tornado-like energy that is frozen inside and trying to release (#5). The energy continues to be generated by thoughts and memories of what happened. When we can be helped to discharge this energy through letting ourselves shake or cry and using releasing techniques in Chapter 5, many post-traumatic reactions such as nightmares and flashbacks are minimized or resolved.[11]

The problem is that our rational thinking brain often gets in the way. We're afraid that the shaking and overwhelming feelings mean we're "going crazy" or falling apart. So we rigidly "hold ourselves together," suppressing these natural, body-healing responses along with strong emotions such as grief and fear (#7).

The intense, tornado-like undischarged trauma energy behind hyperarousal can also show up as anger or rage directed at whatever or whomever is closest and can be blamed—the rescue squad that didn't respond fast enough, the doctor who should have tried harder, the disaster agency that should be providing more assistance, the spouse who isn't empathic enough, the ethnic group of the attackers (#6). Whether the anger is justified or not, its intensity is frequently out of proportion because of the pent-up trauma energy which keeps us in what Daniel Siegel calls "low mode" (lower brain) instinctual, survival states,[12] down the ladder in mobilization fight/flight, our social engagement system muted. Attacking and blaming may make us feel better temporarily but it doesn't help long-term because more trauma energy is generated, and genuine change not achieved.

Anna describes an incident that happened soon after her brother's memorial service, which took place about two months after his death in the World Trade Center.

I was feeling shaky, so I drove to a park to take a walk. A man was there with two dogs, and I asked him to put them on a leash. He told me I needed to be on a leash. I got so angry. I don't know what was in me, but I got into my car and I wanted the engine to ROAR for me. I wanted to plow through the whole known universe. But even the universe wasn't enough. I wanted to roar on out into space, into the galaxy and nebulae and on into the void.

In everyday language, we might say that Anna "lost it." Physiologically, that's accurate. The "it" Anna temporarily lost, to some extent, was her social engagement system/connecting brain function as she swiftly plunged down the ladder into mobilization.

Likely we can all identify moments like this in our own lives. Our ability to regulate our emotions is diminished. So are all the other connecting brain functions: the ability to "read" the nonverbal communication cues of others, take in information from the world around us, reflect on that information before acting, modulate fear, be flexible, feel empathy for others, act with morality for the larger good, and access intuitive "ways of knowing that fuel wisdom."[13] Rational thought is hijacked. We experience intense emotions, impulsive reactions, and rigid and repetitive responses. Our ability to be self-reflective and to consider another person's or group's point of view is impaired.[14]

In Anna's story, we know her connecting brain reengages when the following occurs:

> Then a little voice inside me said, "Anna, turn the car around. Go home." Somewhere inside of me, there was a witness of what was going on. I was really shaking, but I turned the car around and drove home. I thought, "I need to meditate."

Anna chose to listen to the quiet voice inside her and turn around. Since meditation is one of her usual practices, it helps her body continue to regulate and her social engagement system to come more fully online. Clarity, calm, and connection to herself and others are possible again.

Given the intensity of these trauma responses, it is easy to understand why we feel overwhelmed and out of control. It is easy to understand why we suppress feelings, retreat into emotional numbing, or deny what happened and the effects on us (#3, #4, #7). At first, this can seem like a healthy defense, as it keeps us from becoming overwhelmed or out of control. However, withdrawing and numbing are indicators of freeze that negatively affect our relationships and rob us of the ability to live fully in the present. Addressing trauma, the subject of Chapter 5 (see text box), allows us to process the pain in ways that heal us and the world.

Addressing trauma means:

1. Releasing the physical effects of fight, flight, freeze and collapse from the body/brain to restore access to the social engagement system;
2. Acknowledging the impact of polarizing meaning-making narratives on our beliefs and behaviors and exploring new stories;
3. Working nonviolently to transform relationships and systems to meet basic human needs for security and justice.

Trauma shatters meaning

Traumatic events shatter the world as we know it, leaving us feeling disordered, disempowered, and disconnected from other people and from life. Our response may be anxiety, depression, anger, and a flood of questions: Why us? Where was God? And what is the meaning of life, anyway (#6)?

29

Anna describes her experience:

The anger was so nondescript: it was not about the terrorists, but about the whole system, about where we as a human race have gotten. And I was angry at myself. Because despite all the prayer and meditation I've done, I was reacting like this. At some irrational level I thought, "How can my life up to now have any value, any good, if this is who I am?" My feelings came in waves, but for a long time, I felt like I was on the verge of a nervous breakdown.

The depth of feelings, thoughts, and reactions can be frightening, even overwhelming (#3). The losses—of loved ones, homes, jobs, community, status, and security—lead us to wonder who we are as individuals or nations (#6). When we feel out of control or "unspiritual," we tend to suppress the grief, pain, and questions (#7). Feelings of shame, self-blame, and humiliation are common. So is guilt at surviving when others have died (#8).

Although it is not logical, we may believe we should have been able to prevent or overcome whatever happened, or that if we were somehow better people, we wouldn't feel so bad now. In part, what is at stake is our sense of honor, our dignity. We feel shame that it happened, and that it happened to us (#8). And if we don't understand the normal trauma responses of fight, flight, freeze, and that they happen automatically to help us survive, we may be ashamed of how we responded, or didn't respond. As the reality of our losses breaks through the initial shock and denial, we may feel as though we're on the verge of falling apart or "going crazy" (#9).

Trauma creates needs

Traumagenic situations—whether one-time events or chronic/systemic circumstances—often leave us feeling that we have been victimized and treated unjustly (#11). Justice is a basic human need of individuals and groups who have experienced trauma. Restorative justice work with crime victims has identified some of the "justice needs" on the part of those who have been wronged or harmed.[15] These are needs of most people who have experienced trauma.

Often, the most urgent need is for safety and security. We need to know that steps are being taken to prevent the recurrence of what happened. We also want answers, not only because they give meaning, but because they offer a sense of order and therefore physical, emotional, and spiritual security. If we know who did something and why, for example, it may make life seem a bit more predictable. When we don't get adequate answers, we often turn to simplistic meaning-making narratives and explanations to give a sense of meaning and security. More on these narratives in Chapter 4.

Humans are meaning-making creatures. We find much of our identity and security in the meaning we

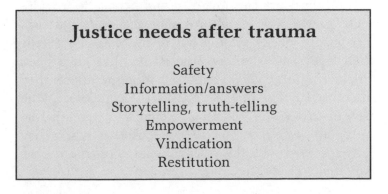

Justice needs after trauma

Safety
Information/answers
Storytelling, truth-telling
Empowerment
Vindication
Restitution

give to the world. These meanings are often embedded in our stories. When trauma shatters our fundamental beliefs and assumptions about life, our stories and belief systems are disrupted (#6). Thus, we look for ways to explain what happened. We may need to "re-story" our lives, revising them in ways that recreate our sense of meaning and identity.

Individuals and groups also need vindication. Partly, this is a moral balancing: we want to know that we are not to blame, that someone else is accepting responsibility. Part of vindication involves releasing the shame and humiliation that accompanies being harmed and, ideally, replacing it with a sense of dignity, honor, and agency.

Sometimes these needs can be addressed, at least in part, by apologies and restitution. If the actual losses are impossible to compensate, some symbolic statement or reparation can help fill this need. Experiences of justice, whether direct or symbolic, often play a critical part in the healing journey of those who have been traumatized. Vicious revenge fantasies are common when our basic human needs for justice are not met (#11).

As noted in Chapter 3, traumagenic events such as natural disasters can magnify and expose to a wider view preexisting structural violence and injustice. The justice needs arising out of traumagenic events then layer onto the systemic issues that have been smoldering and very visible all along to those they affect, even though they are invisible to those who benefit from the existing systems. Although the needs are legitimate, as discussed above, when they are expressed with the volcanic energy of trauma, we can create or add to cycles of violence.

Ongoing trauma

In environments of ongoing trauma, characteristics that would be considered unhealthy in the months after a single traumatic event can be signs of adaptive, survival-based coping.[16] For example, hypervigilance can keep us alive in a high crime neighborhood, when living under military occupation, or while on patrol in a war zone. Emotional numbing and denial help to keep hopelessness and fear at bay, enabling adults to go to work and children to attend school under harrowing circumstances.

While such adaptations may be "normal," they impact our health and well-being. Long-term stress reactions include changes in the way we think about ourselves, the way we perceive those who hurt us, our ability to read social cues, our relations with others, our body's stress response, and our system of meaning. Judith Herman, a physician and trauma expert, says that those who experience single traumas often feel they may be losing their minds, but those who live with long-term trauma often feel they have lost themselves.[17] This loss of identity has serious implications for people's health, the resilience of a society's social fabric, the success of development projects, and the hope of future generations.[18]

> Trauma can either strengthen or undermine a community.

In some situations of ongoing trauma, a strong sense of community develops as people band together to help each other. In Chapter 5, there are examples of people and groups acting well even in the midst of threat. The opposite can also happen, especially when conditions drag on or worsen.

Large-group trauma

Large group traumas that directly impact entire groups or societies include natural disasters, human-caused accidents, and acts of deliberate harm—or a combination of these crises. Hurricane Katrina, which struck the southern US in 2005, is an example of a natural disaster that also involved failure of the surge-protection levees and bungled government responses that affected lower-income, largely African American neighborhoods. Even the disaster planning was blind to the needs of the poorest community members. School buses sat unused while the residents who couldn't afford cars were left stranded. This neglect is not a fluke or aberration as evidenced by the inadequate response to the lead contamination in the Flint, Michigan water supply or Hurricane Maria in Puerto Rico. Environmental racism and injustice are real problems that traumatize many.

Psychiatrist Vamik Volkan has spent several decades working with sociopolitical conflicts of large groups and studying the effects of large-group trauma on present and future societies in various parts of the world. He describes the common reactions to natural disasters as shock, chaos, survivor guilt, and preoccupation with images of death and destruction, which often last for months or even years. Survivors experience a lingering, shared anxiety from having lost trust in "Mother Nature." After a time of mourning, regeneration takes place.[19] Clearly, the magnitude and nature of the disaster affects how long this process takes.

In disasters caused by human failures—the radioactive leakage at Chernobyl, or the collapse of a poorly constructed apartment building—blame is often placed on a small number of individuals, a corporation, or governmental organizations. Although others bear some culpability, and greed or neglect may have been involved, it makes a difference to us if we believe that no one *deliberately* sought to cause harm to us personally. Damage settlements help victims to feel a sense of vindication.[20]

According to Volkan, the most difficult traumas are those deliberately caused by others.[21] The cruelty of calculated harm impacts us intensely. Similarly, Jennifer Freyd and colleagues have found that when people or institutions we know and trust traumatize us, these wounds are especially profound and deep.[22] Frequently, these traumas lead to a predictable series of countermoves from the targets/victims that can start cycles of violence. We respond with fear, rage, helplessness, humiliation, increased group identity, and a desire for vindication. When our basic human need for justice is not met, we may seek revenge.

> The most difficult traumas are those deliberately caused by others.

Deliberate acts of harm often become "chosen traumas," not in the sense that people want terrible things to happen, but that a shared traumatic event is "chosen" to be kept alive through the generations, and becomes an integral part of an individual's or group's identity and narratives. Chosen traumas are characterized by an obsessive sense of being wronged by the "other" and by a sense of entitlement.[23]

Individuals and groups in these states are down the ladder from their social engagement system, reacting from the lower brain in the mobilization mode of fight/ flight, or mired in the powerlessness of immobilization. These aftereffects of trauma bring us to the next chapter: Cycles of Violence from Unaddressed Trauma.

> The past is never dead.
> In fact, it's not even past.
> —Novelist William Faulkner in *Requiem for a Nun*

4.
Cycles of Violence from Unaddressed Trauma:
STAR Model Part II

"Pain that is not transformed is transferred."[1]
—*Richard Rohr, OFM*

When trauma, whether from terrorism or tsunamis, shatters our security, or when we commit to working to right structural harms, we stand at a crossroad. We can choose to address trauma and transform our suffering into something restorative, even a gift to the world. This is the focus of Chapter 5.

In this chapter, however, we examine the road we too frequently find ourselves on by default: trauma is not addressed, and the initial normal reactions morph into destructive cycles of victimhood and/or violence, adding to the suffering of the planet. The

Safety and Security

In some languages, the word for safety and security is the same. In English, the words are sometimes used interchangeably. But there are subtle differences.

Safe/safety is more personal. The polyvagal theory describes our relationships with others, and in the environment around us.

Security suggests freedom from worry that comes from knowing certain external safeguards are in place. We speak of national security, the ways governments protect their own citizens. Or human security, which the United Nations describes as people-centered initiatives to eliminate the drivers of insecurity and ensure that all are free from fear, want, and indignity.

loss of an individual or group's sense of safety can lead to personal or national actions and reactions that lead to the loss of safety and security for others. Examples abound in the news headlines and in the repetitive stories individuals or groups tell of illness, loss, betrayal, an attack, or war. The themes of these grievance stories are suffering, injustice, fear, hopelessness, powerlessness, shame, humiliation, rage, retaliation, and hatred.

What happened is real. The wounds are real. But our responses to trauma can keep us stuck in the pain and fuel deadly tit-for-tat cycles of violence that last for months, years, and even centuries. Part II of the STAR model, Cycles of Violence (page 41–43), examines some of the complex contributing factors. Before looking at the model, however, a word about the commonly used Western framework for understanding unhealed trauma: post-traumatic stress disorder (PTSD).

Limitations of defining unhealed trauma through a PTSD framework

Post-traumatic stress disorder (PTSD) is a diagnosis given to individuals by medical and mental health professionals when reactions or symptoms of trauma related to the event last longer than one month. They include: (1) recurrent, involuntary, intrusive, distressing recollections of what happened (including nightmares, flashbacks, and physical reactivity); (2) persistent avoidance of stimuli associated with the trauma; (3) negative changes in thinking and mood (including self-blame, shame, withdrawing from life, difficulty feeling positive emotions); and (4) changes in arousal and reactivity resulting from the traumatic event (for example, increased irritability, aggressive behavior against the self or others, hypervigilance).[2]

Although PTSD is a helpful description in naming and normalizing the aftereffects of traumatic events, there is ongoing discussion as to how appropriate this Western diagnosis is in large-scale events, situations of ongoing trauma, and across all cultures. It is generally accepted that a small percentage of a population will have severe reactions and need mental health care after disasters. But some experts view the broad use of a PTSD diagnosis as pathologizing normal responses to traumagenic situations.

There is also a danger that trauma responses may be *underestimated* and therefore minimized if PTSD is the standard by which traumatic impact is measured, especially at a collective level. As we saw earlier, trauma impacts brain/body, mind, and spirit. Amidst ongoing trauma or in the wake of a traumagenic event, individuals and groups may appear calm and "normal" with only short-term post-traumatic reactions, or none at all.

Human beings are enormously resilient, and many will genuinely cope well. However, individuals and groups may be experiencing a frozen numbness (hypoarousal) or be alternating between hypo and hyperarousal. The "proof" that people are coping well is not only the absence of classic post-traumatic stress symptoms, nor is it the ability to continue basic activities such as going to work or school. The real indicator is the *quality of our relationships* with ourselves and each other in the months, years, and centuries after a trauma.

> The proof that people are coping well after traumagenic events is not only the absence of classic post-traumatic stress symptoms. It is the quality of our relationships in the ensuring months, years, and centuries.

The beliefs and behavior of individuals, groups, and societies help us understand the full impact of traumatic events and times. Public health statistics for variables such as substance abuse, depression, anxiety, gun violence, and immune disorders, along with PTSD rates, are indicators of the true impact of traumagenic events. A major epidemiological study in the

United States, Adverse Childhood Experiences (ACE), found a strong correlation between trauma before age 18 and adult health and social problems.[3] Likely many never had a PTSD diagnosis. If you recognize these behaviors in yourself, your family, organization, community, or nation, a current or historical trauma may be at the root. These behaviors are part of the cycles of violence from unaddressed trauma.

Cycles of violence model—acting in and acting out trauma[4]

Cycles of violence are not inevitable responses to traumagenic events. They can be prevented, minimized, or interrupted by knowing how to address trauma. But they are exceedingly common when trauma has not been addressed (#1). In fact, Volkan speaks of acting out types of reactions as "the rituals of large group psychology" that come into play where there are ethnic, national, or religious conflicts, hostilities, or wars.[5]

The sense of victimhood may also stem from historic or childhood events or arise under the duress of economic, political, and social instability. It may come when the pride and identity of a secure group is punctured by a provocative threat or surprise attack (#1, #2). It happens when groups benefiting from unjust systems—whether they consciously own their privilege or not—hear less powerful groups challenge those structures (#8).

The Cycles of Violence model on page 42 depicts the process of individuals and groups turning unaddressed trauma energy against the self (Victim Cycle: Acting In) and/or out against others (Aggressor Cycle: Acting Out). Notice that the Victim Cycle is identical

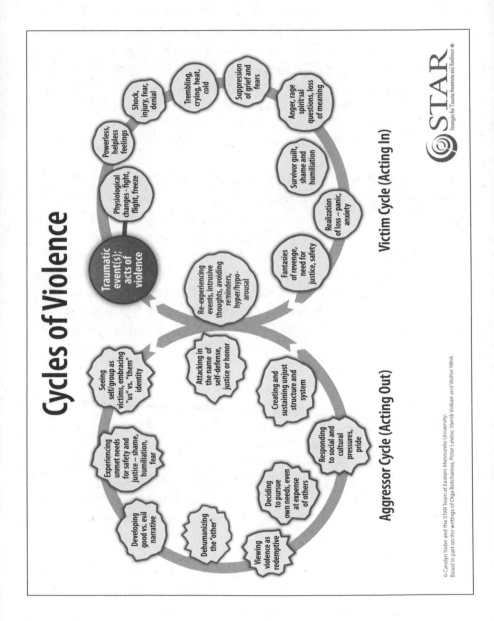

Cycles of Violence

Victim Cycle (Acting In)

Shock, injury, fear, denial

Trembling, crying, heat, cold

Suppression of grief and fears

Anger, rage spiritual questions, loss of meaning

Powerless, helpless feelings

Survivor guilt, shame and humiliation

Physiological changes - fight, flight, freeze

Realization of loss – panic, anxiety

Traumatic event(s); acts of violence

Re-experiencing events, intrusive thoughts, avoiding reminders, hyper/hypo-arousal

Fantasies of revenge, need for justice, safety

Aggressor Cycle (Acting Out)

Seeing self/group as victims, embracing "us" vs. "them" identity

Attacking in the name of self-defense, justice or honor

Creating and sustaining unjust structure and system

Experiencing unmet needs for safety and justice – shame, humiliation, fear

Responding to social and cultural pressures, pride

Developing good vs. evil narrative

Deciding to pursue own needs, even at expense of others

Dehumanizing the "other"

Viewing violence as redemptive

STAR
Strategies for Trauma Awareness and Resilience

© Carolyn Yoder and the STAR Team at Eastern Mennonite University.
Based in part on the writings of Olga Botcharova, Peter Levine, Vamik Volkan and Walter Wink.

to Part I of the model (Trauma Experience), except for the distressed shape of the content bubbles, illustrating that normal trauma responses morph into unhealthy behaviors if trauma is left unaddressed. People can be stuck and spin in the Victim Cycle indefinitely. They can cross the line and become victim-turned-aggressors, creating more victims. They can spin indefinitely in the aggressor cycle. They can swing back and forth between being victimized and acting out as an aggressor.

The Aggressor Cycle/Acting Out may seem at first glance to relate to situations such as terrorist attacks or ethnic violence, but similar dynamics can play in those experiencing structural violence, or going through a bitter divorce, and in conflicts that arise in the aftermath of natural disasters. Although it follows a more predictable progression than the Trauma Experience, few situations are neatly linear. The numbers on each of the points on the model are for ease of reference in the discussion below.

Reenactment behaviors and trigger events

Another name for the patterns of behaviors in the Cycles of Violence model is reenactment. The Examples of Reenactment Behaviors chart on page 44 lists examples of acting in and acting out behaviors that indicate distress from unaddressed trauma. Many are secondary problems that often are treated as primary psychological disorders, with the underlying trauma not recognized or addressed.

Traumatized individuals and groups often have a predominant way of expressing their trauma, some displaying more acting in behaviors (indicating a constricted, *hypo*aroused nervous system) and others

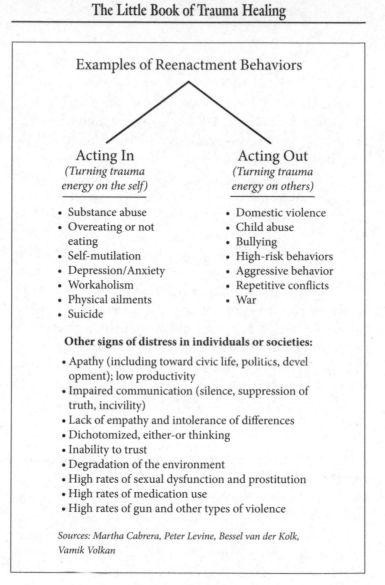

Examples of Reenactment Behaviors

Acting In	Acting Out
(Turning trauma energy on the self)	*(Turning trauma energy on others)*
• Substance abuse	• Domestic violence
• Overeating or not eating	• Child abuse
• Self-mutilation	• Bullying
• Depression/Anxiety	• High-risk behaviors
• Workaholism	• Aggressive behavior
• Physical ailments	• Repetitive conflicts
• Suicide	• War

Other signs of distress in individuals or societies:

• Apathy (including toward civic life, politics, development); low productivity
• Impaired communication (silence, suppression of truth, incivility)
• Lack of empathy and intolerance of differences
• Dichotomized, either-or thinking
• Inability to trust
• Degradation of the environment
• High rates of sexual dysfunction and prostitution
• High rates of medication use
• High rates of gun and other types of violence

Sources: Martha Cabrera, Peter Levine, Bessel van der Kolk, Vamik Volkan

more aggressive acting out behaviors (indicating a *hyper*aroused nervous system). However, often there is a swing back and forth between hypo and hyper arousal. For example, a person who is withdrawn and depressed may suddenly erupt into rage at slight triggers.

Reenactment behaviors represent attempts to numb or resolve trauma.[6] They often (unconsciously) intensify around the anniversary of the traumatic event. A seemingly minor event—a smell, sound, gesture, tone of voice, fleeting memory, group dynamic, symbol— can trigger an intrusive reaction or a conscious or unconscious memory that propels us into a low-mode brain reaction. The longer trauma is unaddressed, the greater the likelihood that the "fire-together-wire-together" neural pathways will strengthen, where reacting to triggers becomes our default way of being.

Impaired body/brain functioning

As discussed in Chapter 3, trauma disrupts the ability of the connecting brain to help us function as thoughtful, creative, emotionally intelligent individuals and societies. When we are hypo or hypervigilant from unaddressed or ongoing trauma, brain functioning is impacted, and we interpret even the benign actions of others as threats.

Stephen Porges's Polyvagal Theory advances our understanding of this interaction between the brain and the body's social nervous system. He found that when neuroception alerts us that something in our bodies, the environment, or an interaction with others doesn't feel safe, we subconsciously read neutral faces as aggressive and fearful faces as angry. By contrast, when we are relaxed, we use our faces and voices to negotiate relationships and maintain safety in thoughtful ways. All this happens below our level of consciousness.[7]

Neurobiology research has primarily focused on individuals, not groups or societies. However, both Martha Cabrera's and Vamik Volkan's descriptions of societies dealing with large-scale or ongoing traumas are strikingly parallel to Siegel's description of individuals with impaired middle prefrontal cortical function, that is, the connecting brain. In Chapter 3, we saw that when we're at the top of the ladder, the face-heart social engagement system/connecting brain enables us to regulate emotions (including the fear responses of the limbic system fight/flight), respond flexibly, experience empathy for the pain of others, be self-aware, access our intuition and innate wisdom, and act ethically and altruistically. By contrast, in Cabrera's Nicaragua, after decades of conflict, she describes a reduced ability to communicate, reduced ability to be flexible and tolerant, and a loss of trust between people. She also described apathy, isolation, aggressiveness, chronic illness, increases in domestic violence and suicide, and an inability to see history through the eyes of another.[8]

Volkan has observed that societies with extensive trauma and conflict typically exhibit what John Mack has called the "egoism of victimization,"[9] that is, a reduction in their ability to see beyond their own pain and to empathize with the suffering of others. Consequently, they experience little guilt about committing retaliatory violence or contributing to cycles of violence (#9) and fail to take responsibility for the victims and suffering created by their own actions[10] (#6, #7). This dynamic can be observed whether the issue is an international conflict or something more personal, like a bitter divorce.

The behaviors indicate distress, dis-ease, and reenactment of trauma at the individual and collective level.

Incomplete grieving and mourning

Tears are a way to release trauma energy and break through the immobility, numbness, or suppression that at first defended us from unbearable pain. Healthy grieving (internal emotions and thoughts) and mourning (external rituals and the process of adjusting to the loss) are key to moving toward healing, whether from the death of a loved one, the effects of terrorism, the legacy of cultural genocide, or the chaos left in the wake of natural disasters. However, the process frequently gets thwarted for several reasons.

> There is no greater agony
> than bearing an untold story inside of you.
> —Poet Maya Angelou

First, if traumagenic events are ongoing, the focus is on emotional and physical survival as concerns for day-to-day safety and security supersede all else.

Second, when there is destruction of buildings and infrastructure, as after an earthquake or war, by necessity the emphasis is on providing the basics of food, shelter, and health care for months or even years. When schools reopen and the hospitals and bridges are rebuilt, people often want normal routines to resume and to focus forward rather than spending time thinking about the painful past. In the attempt to "get over it" and move on, grief is suppressed.

Third, when we let go of numbness and denial, the intensity of emotions—humiliation, rage, fear, despair—can feel overwhelming, even like death. Feeling or expressing them feels too risky. Anger often smolders just beneath the surface. This bottled-up rage blocks the ability to feel grief, complicating the ability to move forward.

Fourth, we cannot grieve or mourn what we will not acknowledge. Perhaps "our side" has "lost"—or lost face. Or perhaps we have "won," but we fear that mourning somehow means the other side has triumphed (#7). Sometimes, knowing the truth about what happened can seem to destroy the last shred of hope.

Fifth, acknowledgment of what happened is an exercise in truth-telling which can threaten the social, economic, or political order (#8). For example, families frequently minimize a substance abuse problem or turn against a member who exposes sexual assault. At a societal level, those who seek to bring a country's atrocities or less-than-honorable events or policies to light are labeled unpatriotic. Worse, the truth-bearers may be discredited, silenced, or even murdered (#7).

Sixth, sometimes it is not possible to know what happened. Crimes go unsolved, soldiers disappear without explanation, people commit suicide, detainees are held incognito. Such situations create what social scientist Pauline Boss calls "ambiguous grief" or "frozen sadness" for the surviving loved ones and the wider society.[11] Even if people want to know the truth, information is sometimes available only incrementally as facts become available.

Seventh, mourning can also be impacted by not having the physical body of a loved one. When a plane plunges into the ocean or people are buried in mass graves because of epidemics or genocide, it robs loved ones of the opportunity to carry out the usual cultural and religious rituals.

Anna shares from her story:

As soon as they allowed planes to fly again, I went back to New York. We went through what to do when there are no remains. I framed it that my brother was basically cremated, and I don't have a problem with cremation. But even so, it affected me. No body, no gravesite. It must be one of the most difficult things people face worldwide, when someone dies far from home, or there's a mass burial, or there are no remains.

Obstacles to grieving and mourning

- Trauma that is ongoing
- Not wanting to look back
- Fear of being overwhelmed
- Inability to face what happened
- Threats to the known "order"
- Truth is unknowable
- Inability to carry out usual rituals

Regardless of the reasons why grieving and mourning are incomplete, the resulting frozen and suppressed emotions thwart healing and keep people more susceptible to low-mode brain states.

Frozen grief thwarts healing.

Normal fear easily morphs into panic or paranoia, pain into despair, anger into rage, and humiliation and shame turn into an obsessive drive for vindication. The quest to meet our basic need for justice is then confused with retaliation and revenge. These patterns and frustrations are intensified if the justice needs described in Chapter 3 are not met. Even more frightening, we as individuals and groups are more susceptible to meaning-making narratives that can lead us from being victims/survivors to aggressors.

Meaning-making narratives shaping our beliefs and cycle of violence behaviors

When trauma shatters our world, or keeps us living in fear, we tell stories and construct narratives to explain what happened and make meaning of life. Under the duress of threat, fear, grief, and unmet needs for justice and security, we unconsciously latch onto familiar narratives which shape our beliefs and behaviors:

- Good vs. evil
- Us vs. them
- Chosen trauma
- Redemptive violence (violence is necessary for security)

Good-versus-evil narratives provide a sense of vindication (#3) and allow the "good" side (which is me/my group) to project unwanted characteristics onto the "evil" side, the enemy who is often stripped of human goodness[12] (#4). Projecting evil onto the "other" shifts the attention away from the "good" side's own shortcomings. It blinds us to our contribution to the conflict and our own dysfunctions or internal societal ills. The "other" becomes the focus and scapegoat.

50

Leaders, media, and unreflective citizens can sustain good-versus-evil narratives until they take on a life of their own. What happened may then become the "chosen trauma" for either side, an event or series of events around which an individual or group organizes its identity. Once embedded in a psyche or a culture, a chosen trauma narrative is difficult to dispel. Regardless of the origins, the more the security of a group is threatened or shattered, the more tightly we as humans cling to group identity, becoming suspicious of or openly hostile to those who are different from us (#6).

Some politicians deliberately create or exacerbate the breakdown of trust and promote polarizing narratives. A sense of "us" versus "them" develops or deepens and is expressed through patriotic or "in-group" symbols such as flags, songs, dress, food, and other customs (#1).

> When politicians promote an "us" versus "them" mentality, truth becomes the first casualty.

In such an atmosphere, truth becomes the first casualty. Facts are twisted, motivations embellished, and heroes and villains created. Challenging the narrative is seen as unpatriotic and even as betrayal of one's group (#6, #7).

When an individual, group, or nation buys into a good-versus-evil narrative, demonizing and then dehumanizing of the "other" easily follows (#4). Labels such as "terrorist," "bad," "criminals," "unpatriotic," "traitor," and "infidel" are interwoven with descriptors like inhuman, insane, animals, and barbaric. When the "other" is dehumanized and made

51

evil, then moral standards based on the sanctity of life no longer apply (#6). Torture is sanctioned, and the usual rule-of-law standard is put aside. A dangerously simplistic analysis with an equally simplistic solution gains momentum: if the cause of the threat is evil people or groups, the solution is to separate them from us—or even kill them (#9)—in the name of our just cause.

Aren't some things truly evil?

At this point, you may be wondering, "But what about victims of the Holocaust? The Nakba? The Doctrine of Discovery which led to the decimation of Aboriginal peoples? Jim Crow laws that enforced racial segregation in the US for nearly a century and whose legacy continues? Genocide? Weaponized rape? Human trafficking? And that bully who made my life miserable in high school?

Isn't there evil in the world? Times where there is clearly a good side and evil side? Times when retreating with one's in-group is necessary to save a culture and people threatened with annihilation? To build solidarity necessary to work for justice?

Yes. And read on.

STAR was created as a response to 9/11. Every situation may not fit neatly in the model. But notice what does apply, even to the "good" side.

Being the victim, the innocent, the survivor, the oppressed group, does not mean we have no work to do. It doesn't exempt us from addressing the trauma we carry. Otherwise, we unreflectively can cross a line, and, in the words of international conflict resolution expert Olga Botcharova, we become "yesterday's victims who are today's aggressors." Aggressors in the way we work for justice. In the spirit we carry toward others in our hearts. Even in how we treat our own children.

The common narrative underlying this belief and behavior is the ancient myth of redemptive violence: violence must be used to overcome violence (#5). Violence has the power to make us secure, keep us free, and restore a sense of pride and honor.[13] Lam, who survived the bus attack in Uganda, recalls:

The feeling of "chosen trauma" . . . has engulfed whole communities and tribes. They justify acts of revenge for their victimization and identify fellow citizens as "the other" who deserve their suffering. For instance, most people felt justified in using scorched-earth military tactics because "we too suffered at their hands." All Northerners were labeled "anya-nya," killers who deserve to be killed. Many innocent people were killed in the cruelest way, being burnt alive with car tires around their necks.[14]

As author Gil Bailie and others have suggested, the narrative of redemptive violence can be applied to the future, justifying violence to be perpetrated against "the other." This narrative can also be applied to the past, justifying and helping to explain our previous actions.[15] The egoism of victimization is in full play (#6).

> In people's experience, what happened centuries ago have echoes in what happened last week.
> —Douglas R. Baker[16]

The role of leaders

Threat and security are real issues that must be addressed by groups and nations. But as we have seen, when leaders and citizens alike are hypervigilant and emotions run high, it is frequently difficult to determine the true measure of threat. Volkan says the role of leaders is pivotal at such junctures: they hold the potential to enflame (destructive leaders) or tame (reparative leaders). He cites twenty signs of large group regression, the fallout of fear and anxiety from traumagenic events whether natural disasters, economic factors, terrorism, or war.[17] Two of the most predictable are that (1) group members lose their individuality as they rally blindly around a central leader, and (2) the splits between good/bad and us/them intensify. Those labeled "them" are often scapegoated and demonized.

Malignant regression occurs when leaders themselves are also regressed, along with their citizens, and people are killed, or lives ruined.[18] Although their actions may not be intentional or conscious, destructive and malignant leaders escalate anxiety and fear by:

- magnifying dangers;
- blurring reality and fantasy;

- barraging the public with constant reminders of vague, looming threats;
- manipulating by withholding, distorting, or misrepresenting facts, goals, and situations;
- engaging in name-calling;
- labeling dissenting views unpatriotic or traitorous;
- dehumanizing by using "us/them" and "good/evil" dichotomies.

> Perceptions often matter as much as truth.

Perception matters as much as truth when it comes to group response and willingness to follow such leaders (#7). The late Louise Diamond, cofounder of the Institute for Multi-Track Diplomacy, describes this phenomenon:[19]

I have watched political leaders all over the world use fear to manipulate the people. It is a common tactic, one of whose outcomes is to ensure that those in power stay in power. It plays to the lowest tones of human consciousness rather than to the highest. To keep the people hypnotically caught in a fog of fear is to keep them helpless, thereby undermining democracy and preventing the evolution of human society and spirit.

Traumatized individuals, groups, and nations play out these ancient narratives as if asleep, unaware of the mythic drama that is unfolding. Regardless of whether we call it living unconsciously, lower brain function, collective denial, trauma reenactment, sin, or group-think, the end result is the same: an attack against "the other" is justified in the name of self-defense, justice, security, honor, or freedom (#9).

But the security we yearn, fight, and die for is rarely the long-term outcome. Physical or psychological violence/war, even within the parameters of a righteous cause, a patriotic cause, a just war, a holy war, leaves in its wake more people and societies that experience trauma and are humiliated, hypervigilant, angry, fearful, grieving, and feeling profoundly unsafe (#1, #2). Victims have become aggressors, in the process creating more victims with their own heightened sense of group identity, their own good-versus-evil narratives (#3), and their own needs for justice and vindication (#2). These new victims/survivors fuel new enemy/aggressor cycles of violence. And thus, another tit-for-tat story, like those that fill our media every day, begins anew. Lam says:

> *Violence was institutionalized as a response to political issues that required dialogue and understanding. The desire for revenge only perpetuated the violence.*

The cycle across generations

Contrary to the popular adage, time does not heal all wounds. Unhealed trauma is passed from generation to generation in families, communities, and nations. It is acted *in* through depression,

Time does not heal all wounds.

anxiety, substance abuse, and suicide. It is acted *out* on the family through domestic and child abuse, and on the community and society through the violent cycles described in the sections above.

Succeeding generations bear the brunt of the frozen grief and acting in and acting out behaviors of the elders. In addition, they may be given "shared tasks"—the unfinished business of their parents—such as continually grieving their ancestors' losses, feeling their victimization, striving for justice, or getting revenge. The common denominator in all these shared tasks is to keep the large group's memories alive. Generally, these tasks cannot be effectively dealt with by the next generation, so they are passed on to yet another generation, sometimes in a changed form.[20]

How can individuals and societies avoid getting stuck in the cycle of victimhood and violence? How do leaders, trauma-impacted along with their citizens, provide for both short- and long-term security, yet not set in motion tit-for-tat cycles of violence?

In the next chapter, we examine the third part of the STAR model, Breaking Cycles of Violence: Building Resilience. If lived out, it has the potential to interrupt cycles of violence and reduce or even prevent future violence.

5.
Breaking Cycles of Violence and Building Resilience:
STAR Model Part III

"I have looked into the abyss of human evil and seen the depth to which we can plumb. But paradoxically . . . you encounter people who, having suffered grievously, should by right be riddled with bitterness and lust for revenge and retribution. But they are different."
—Archbishop Emeritus Desmond Mpilo Tutu[1]

Part III of the Breaking Cycles of Violence/ Building Resilience STAR model, shown on page 62, is a compass for addressing trauma in nonviolent ways that transform relationships and meet basic human needs for security and justice. The ideas presented here are neither perfected nor complete. They are simply part of the quest to find effective and life-giving ways to heal personal and collective trauma.

Moving beyond fight, flight, freeze/collapse reactions requires attention to the brain/body, mind, heart, and spirit. Peter Levine speaks of the resilience, creativity, cooperative spirit, and sense of triumph experienced by those who address and transform trauma.[2] Martha Cabrera describes the need for "affective and spiritual reconstruction" for individuals, communities, and societies that have experienced violence.[3] Paula Gutlove, who founded a program that links public health and conflict resolution, points out the importance of psychosocial healing, that is, engaging in psychological and social-support activities that help populations function in stable and healthy ways in the wake of conflict.[4] Psychologist and STAR trainer Donna Minter, founder of the Minneapolis Peacebuilding Leadership Institute, calls us to transform the energy of trauma into nonviolent power rather than using it to fuel cycles of violence.[5]

Most of us are familiar with nonviolence as a means to work for social change but have only a cursory sense of the broad range of situations in which it can be used, the preparation, skills, and strategies it requires (conflict analysis, negotiation, coalition building, the strategic sequencing of nonviolent direct action tactics, the ability to attract wide participation to the movement, and to resolve disputes, among others);[6] and its demonstrated effectiveness. Award-winning scholars Erica Chenoweth and Maria J. Stephan conducted a statistical analysis of 323 violent and nonviolent civil resistance campaigns in over 140 countries between 1900 and 2006. They found that groups who used nonviolent civil resistance to pursue their goals of regime change or expulsion of foreign occupiers were twice as successful in achieving their goals as groups who waged violent resistance campaigns, even when dealing with harsh regimes.[7] (Updated figures that include 1900 to 2015 show nonviolent campaigns succeeded 51 percent of the time; violent campaigns 27 percent.[8]) A key reason for the success of nonviolent movements was "their ability to attract large and diverse participation"—women, the elderly, children, and persons with disabilities—in fact, eleven times more participants than violent campaigns.

Chenoweth and Stephan found a stable democracy was more likely to take root after a successful nonviolent campaign. By contrast, after a violent campaign, civil war is more likely to break out within ten years.[9] And consider this surprising finding: the average nonviolent campaign took three years to achieve its goals; the average violent campaign took nine.[10] In Liberia, Nepal, and Colombia, broad-based nonviolent movements successfully pressured warring parties to end deadly civil wars.[11]

Chenoweth and Stephan also analyzed why some nonviolent movements failed—for example, internal divisions among leaders, inadequate training and support in nonviolent tactics, and lack of a creative strategy to maintain the resistance in the face of repression.[12] And Chenoweth cautions that even when movements avoid violence, attract wide participation, and are skillful and strategic in their tactics, regimes can sew disunity, which can be deadly. She warns, whichever side splinters their opposition most effectively ("divide and rule") wins.[13]

In our STAR trainings, we witness a hunger in participants for ways to respond to differences and threats that do not rely on attacking other groups (fight), passively avoiding or accomodating them (flight), or disengaging (freeze). The civil society leaders in our trainings know firsthand the devastating effects of violence and trauma. We believe that all of us would be more secure if even a portion of the intellectual and financial resources that now go into preparing for warfare were devoted to: (1) understanding trauma, the cycles of violence, and body/brain release; (2) educating all of us—including our leaders—to recognize when we are making decisions from a hyper or hypo aroused lower brain rather than with the social engagement system/connecting brain; and (3) training military personnel and civilians in strategic nonviolence strategies *before* a crisis happens.

Understanding the model

Before reading the next section, I recommend that you examine the Breaking Cycles diagram on page 62. The two small inner cycles are an abbreviated version of Parts I and II of the model, Trauma Experience and the Cycles of Violence. The broken lines suggest that it is possible to break out of these cycles at any time and that the diagram is not linear. The wavelike design running throughout the snail shape indicates the importance of interweaving body-brain regulating exercises every step of the way to increase the efficacy and effectiveness of the healing tools and processes.

Like the other parts of the model, this two-dimensional diagram cannot capture the dynamic complexity of addressing trauma in ways that work for lasting security and changing systems. Also, the discussion that follows may seem to jump from the personal

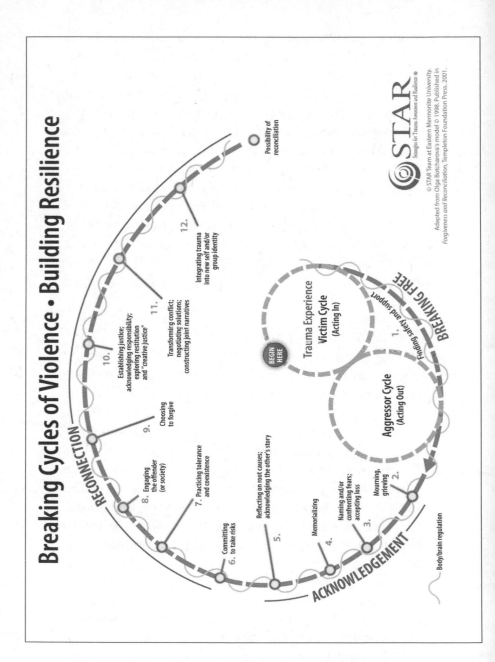

to the collective. This is because the two are inter-twined—the personal is often communal or social, and vice versa.

The "points" on the outer cycle are numbered, again, not because the process is linear, but for ease of reference. The snail/galaxy shape itself is meta-phoric: the process may be snail-like, taking months, years, or even decades; or it may be galaxy-like, lead-ing us to places previously thought unimaginable. A detailed explanation of all these interrelated points is beyond the scope of this book, but all fall under the three main general headings, which we will discuss below: Breaking Free (Safety), Acknowledgment, and Reconnection.[14,15]

Breaking Free: *Safety (#1) in a traumagenic world*

Safety is foundational to trauma healing. It is a powerful antidote to threat and fear,[16] increasing the possibility of breaking free of the cycles of violence. This is not surprising given that when we feel safe, our social engagement system and connecting brain are online. Indeed, it has often been said that safety is a precondition for addressing trauma.

But this line of thinking leads to a conundrum: given unjust systems, ongoing threats, and the con-flict and violence in our world, how can we wait until there is safety before addressing trauma, since unhealed trauma contributes to cycles of victimhood and violence? So can we have safety, security, and peace without trauma healing? How can we work at healing even though there is no peace?

Most of us know people who respond in compassionate, life-giving ways despite trauma, danger, or reasons to retaliate. Jewish psychiatrist Viktor Frankl experienced inner freedom in a Nazi concentration camp.[17] In 1999, Lam Cosmas became head of the Acholi Religious Leaders Peace Initiative, an interfaith organization of Muslim and Christian leaders committed to peacebuilding in this still-unstable region of Uganda. Mary Anderson and Marshall Wallace document thirteen communities around the world who developed creative strategies that kept them out of wars that engulfed neighboring villages.[18]

What loosens the grip of the fight, flight, freeze and collapse responses in individuals and communities, allowing profound acts of courage and compassion to blossom in the midst of threat and insecurity? What releases them from neuroception-driven stories and the lower brain's instinct to act only for its own survival?

In peacebuilding workshops in the former Yugoslavia, participants reflected on times when they had been under threat and, by conventional reasoning, had "the right" to attack or strike back. Muslims, Christians, and those of no religious faith reported strikingly similar experiences: "small secret doubts" had surfaced about the rightness of the retaliatory actions they were contemplating. When they chose to follow "the still small voice" and not carry out their plans, they realized a profound truth: the worst evil is not death; the worst evil is betraying the soul by ignoring the inner voice. Consequently, they discovered they lost their fear of death and experienced a significant sense of connection "with the source of spiritual power." Acting well in spite of threat released them from fear.[19]

Such experiences point to our ability to act in ways beyond basic survival instincts, even when complete physical safety is not assured. Perhaps our traditional thinking about safety needs to be reframed with new questions:

- What *degree* of safety?
- What *kind* of safety?

What if being rooted socially in a community, and grounded emotionally, psychologically, and spiritually with a Source beyond ourselves creates a safe space— an inner space, a heart space, a wisdom space—that allows healing to begin even without physical safety? What if practices such as deep breathing, mindfulness, prayer, and working with the body's energy system can lower hyperarousal and move us up the nervous system ladder out of immobilization and mobilization, and open us to new possibilities, even while under threat? Might knowing our ideals and values, and what we are willing to die for—*but not to kill for*[20]—provide an inner strength that propels us into these deeper spaces beyond fear? Is "acting well in spite of threat" a key to breaking, preventing, and transcending the traumatic cycles of victimhood and violence that undermine long-term security? Does "acting well in spite of threat" surprise and throw the "enemy" off guard, creating a chink in their defensive armor, allowing them to see our humanity, and also profoundly changing us? If so, how do we promote and cultivate this ability, both individually and as societies?

A third way:
neither passivity nor violence

In *The Night of the New Moon*, author Laurens van der Post reflects on his experience in a prisoner-of-war camp in World War II. He recounts the day that one of the crueler camp commanders, infuriated by his inability to extract information from the POW officers, commanded the men to line up. Screaming invectives and breaking a sturdy chair in his rage, he ordered the officers to come forward one by one. Then he and a guard clubbed them with pieces from the chair and kicked them as the others awaited their turn. Standing in line, van der Post noted with alarm how the commander's frenzy grew with each beating, and how his hand repeatedly went to the hilt of the sword at his side.

After van der Post was beaten, he began to hobble to the back of the line when a voice deep inside him "with the authority of life itself" said, "Turn about. Go back and present yourself for another beating." According to van der Post, the voice was so insistent that without hesitation, and defying all rationality, he walked back and once more stood at attention in front of the commander who was ready with his cudgel raised.

It took the commander a moment to realize that the officer in front of him was the same person he had just beaten. He stopped, his eyes registering the shock, his raised hand frozen. Van der Post writes: "I believe it made him suddenly aware of himself as an individual facing, not an abstract and symbolic entity, but another individual being."

> The commander took a half-hearted swipe at van der Post's head and shoved him back toward the line. Then he turned and walked away, the guard at his heels.

Here are some of the factors STAR training participants identified that help create safety even amidst uncertainty and threat:

- Social support from inside and outside the trauma situation
- Using mind-body techniques to counter hyperarousal and allow connecting brain function
- An understanding of trauma and the cycles of violence
- Learning effective nonviolent, nonpassive options for responding to threat before a crisis
- A sustaining faith or spiritual practice
- Positive leaders (see next section)
- An active willingness to move beyond victimhood or violence

Cardiologist Herbert Benson, who founded Harvard's Mind/Body Medical Institute, researched ways to elicit the relaxation response in the body, that is, adjusting to challenges and change by countering the stress response and calming the fight-flight-freeze automatic mobilization reactions internally. These self-regulation exercises, also called body-brain or mind-body tools, allow us to maintain feelings of safety internally even when we aren't receiving cues of safety from another person.[21] They include deep breathing, repetitive exercise, repetitive prayer, meditation, yoga, guided imagery, mindfulness, tai chi, and progressive muscle relaxation.[22] Other activities that people have found helpful include sports, qigong, massage, drumming, singing, journaling, art, and dancing.

Trauma expert Bessel van der Kolk stresses the importance of using both "bottom up" and "top down" experiences to counter the effects of trauma. "Bottom up" refers to body-based methods that allow us to recover from the helplessness, rage, and emotional and physical collapse that result from trauma. "Top down" are cognitive experiences—talking, reasoning, and reconnecting with others.[23]

Applications of Stephen Porges's Polyvagal theory provide ways to recognize the state of our nervous system, befriend it even when it is dysregulated, and use self-regulation and co-regulation to return to center.[24] He points out that our ability to self-regulate is not only about learning skills like yoga, but also comes from the process of co-regulation, that is, the positive impact on our own nervous system that comes from mutual, reciprocal, safe relationships with others. Co-regulation begins when we experience safety with our earliest caregivers and extends throughout life when we feel safe with friends, family, and other groups.[25] It happens as we sing in a choir, play an instrument in a band, or team up for a friendly neighborhood game of basketball or badminton. Porges says that co-regulation is a biological imperative for humans,[26] that is, our survival depends on our ability to provide the degree of safety to each other that positively impacts our physiological state. This explains why dysregulating an individual, group, or society through fear tactics is so dangerous and even deadly.

During her time as a volunteer teacher in Northern Uganda, Esther Harder wrote:

I am using soccer as an antidote to fear. . . . As we bounce around the termite mounds, potholes and saplings trying to score, it is much easier to feel like a normal human being. The soldiers are still at the sidelines, and the helicopters still hover, but during the deafening jubilation after a goal, shoulders loosen from tension and smiles brighten the dusk.[27]

Breaking Free: *Safety and the role of leaders*

In times of crisis and threat, the way national and community leaders—presidents, prime ministers, elders, mayors, clergy, educators, community organizers—interpret events, frame the narrative, and address needs can either inflame the situation further or bring a measure of rationality and calm. This is a form of co-regulation. In contrast to the characteristics of destructive and malignant leaders noted in Chapter 4, Volkan's research also identifies traits of positive or "reparative leaders."[28] They help their people to:

- Separate fantasy from reality and the past from the present.
- Evaluate and face realistic dangers and problem-solve.
- Learn about the humanity of enemy groups/ offenders.
- Hold the tension of paradox.

- Restore ties to families, clans, and other groups that support an individual's reconnection to reality.
- Value freedom of speech and consider what is moral.

Positive leaders, thus, serve as an "auxiliary connecting brain" for the people they lead so they can move up the ladder toward the social engagement system rather than staying in fight/flight mobilization or freeze/collapse immobilization. They help find creative, nonviolent responses to crises that are neither passive nor violent.

But what happens when grassroots and mid-level community leaders themselves are harmed by traumatic events, as in a shared trauma, or are caught up in narrow ethnic or nationalist thinking? Then they, too, would benefit from advice and counsel from counterpart persons or groups outside the circle of impact to help them find responses to the threat that go beyond fight, flight, freeze, or collapse.

In large-group events and conflicts when even national leaders are affected, could allies of the affected country or organizations fill the function of a co-regulating "auxiliary connecting brain:" the North Atlantic Treaty Organization (NATO), the African Union (AU), the Association of South East Asian Nations (ASEAN), the Organization of American States (OAS), or the United Nations (UN)?

> Positive, reparative leaders serve as an auxiliary connecting brain in times of crisis. But when impacted by traumagenic events along with their people, they, too, may need someone to serve as an auxiliary connecting brain for them.

Acknowledgment: *Mourning and grieving what happened to us, and naming fears (#2, #3, #4)*

We now come to acknowledgment, a process at the heart of the healing work required for breaking cycles of violence and building resilience. We will be guided by two sets of questions, one emerging from trauma work in the former Yugoslavia,[29] and the other from Father Michael Lapsley, a New Zealand native who lost both hands and the sight in one eye when a letter bomb was mailed to him while he was working to end apartheid in South Africa. He now works with healing of memories.[30]

Acknowledging what happened to us—telling our story in some form—is essential to healing. Individuals and groups may resist, saying they want to focus on the future and move on. However, without mourning and acknowledgment in some form, grief and trauma come out in unhealthy, destructive cycles of violence. Having the support of family, community, and the culture helps make acknowledgment possible. Sometimes, outside experts can provide the safety needed to release our stories, especially when trust is low.

Lapsley says there are three questions we must address if we are to heal. The first has to do with acknowledging our own story: What was done to me/us? This begins the process of counteracting the isolation, silence, fear, shame, and/or "unspeakable" horror of our trauma. It allows frozen emotions to release. It allows us to grieve and mourn.

Sometimes we want to talk about or even shout out what happened, our history. Other times, the shame and fear of being overwhelmed keeps us silent. Words are not the only way to acknowledge trauma.

71

In fact, a growing number of trauma experts believe that without going beyond words and involving the body/brain in releasing as we talk and express, it is impossible to fully address trauma, find healing, and build a healthy future.[31,32,33,34,35]

Art, music, dance, drama, writing, prayer, cultural rituals, and cleansing ceremonies all are ways to give voice to our stories. Massage and other forms of body work release the tension the nervous system holds from our trauma wounds and can be taught and practiced in community settings.[36] Emotional Freedom Technique (EFT)[37] and Thought Field Therapy (TFT)[38] are two evidence-based ways of working through what happened that require few words and release the trauma energy of troubling memories, emotions, and conflicted thinking. Both practices can be learned and used by almost anyone, including children. The Trauma Release Exercise (TRE)[39] is a way to literally let the body shake off energy and can be done individually or in groups. Many cultures have rituals and ceremonies that provide a way for a similar process to happen in a community setting.

Trauma healers also stress the importance of opening memories gradually to ensure that overwhelming feelings do not plunge us into hyperarousal again.[40,41,42,43,44] Peter Levine offers practical guidance on how to tell our stories in manageable steps, moving between comfort and discomfort in order to gradually deactivate a hyperactive nervous system and avoid re-traumatization.[45] Eye Movement Desensitization and Reprocessing[46] (EMDR), used by mental health professionals, is a gentle and effective technique to deal with troubling memories and flashbacks. Creating a memorial (#4), a concrete symbol of

---

How does body/brain and the release of trauma look applied to collective and structural issues?

A powerful example is *My Grandmother's Hands: Racialized Trauma and the Pathway to Mending our Hearts and Bodies* by activist and licensed social worker Resmaa Menakem. Written for a US audience, it focuses on white people, black/dark people, and public safety professionals such as police.

But Menakem presents principles and tools in Part II (Remembering Ourselves) and Part III (Mending Our Collective Body) that can be applied to a wide range of current and historic traumas anywhere.

Why do Menakem and others believe it will make a difference? Because somatic (body) therapies are proving life-changing for individuals who have experienced trauma. And organizations like Green String Network in East Africa (https://www.green-string.org) are collecting data on the changes from using an adapted, contextualized version of STAR in conflicted countries, communities, and clans. "This work," they say, "makes the intractable possible."

---

trauma and loss, provides a physical place to grieve, and the comfort of knowing what happened is publicly acknowledged and will not be forgotten.

Acknowledgment of what happened to us, and the subsequent grieving and mourning it releases, helps us accept that life will never be the same. Facing the possibility of a "new normal" can bring up a host of fears about the future—fears that must be named and realistically addressed. Otherwise, individuals or groups remain easily susceptible to triggers that send them down the nervous system ladder, throwing them back to the low-mode responses of the victim or aggressor cycles.

Acknowledgment of our story usually doesn't happen all at once but unfolds over months and years. Often part of the story is withheld, either consciously or unconsciously (more on this in the next section). And the process of acknowledgment isn't finished only with facing what happened to us/our group. In fact, the first part of acknowledgment can increase the intensity of "Why me?" or "Why us?" questions. The agony of these aching, universal cries reflects the deep longing to find reason and meaning. Yet repetitively dwelling on these often-unanswerable questions keeps us stuck away from our social engagement system and provokes the greatest anger at everything and everyone associated with the perpetrator.[47]

Participants in the Yugoslavia workshops found it helped to reframe "Why me/us" questions as "Why them? Why did they do it, and why did they do it to me/us?"[48] This opens the way for a search for root causes, a conflict transformation process. It leads to the second part of acknowledgment: recognizing that "the other," the enemy, the abuser also has a story.

Acknowledgment: *Recognizing "the other's" story (#5)*

It's human to stop with acknowledgment of our own story. It is not natural, easy, or comfortable to take the next step where we look at the history of those who hurt us, whether a family member, another racial or ethnic group, or another nation. It takes courage to turn our "Why me/us?" question into curiosity about "the other." It may be the hardest work we as humans ever do.

> Seeking to understand does *not* mean condoning what happened.

Using body/brain self-regulation and co-regulation exercises as individuals or groups when we do the work of acknowledgement helps us consider information that may challenge or contradict our own story and can keep us from quickly becoming defensive (fight) or shutting down (flight or freeze). Be clear that seeking to understand root causes does *not* mean condoning what happened. In the aftermath of 9/11, "Why us?" questions soon were intermingled with "Why do they hate us?" This was a cry for answers, for information to help make sense of what happened.

"Why them?" questions require more than quick, surface answers. They require a deep knowledge of our own history, one that includes views from the margins and our shadow history we may rather ignore. It requires going beyond short media blurbs when you explore the history of "the other." Awareness of decades and even centuries of history may be needed to understand present events. We may never be able to fully understand. But what often emerges is that our enemy, our "other," acted out of the anger, fear, and even the helplessness of being wronged, victimized, and traumatized themselves—sometimes even by us or by our group.

> Moving from asking "Why us?" to asking "Why them? Why did they do it, and why did they do it to me/us?" is conflict transformation work.

This in no way absolves anyone of responsibility for aggression, discrimination, or atrocities. "The other" is responsible for how they chose to respond to their current or historic traumas, just as we are responsible for our actions and reactions when our security is threatened, or we are attacked, mistreated, and harmed.

When we have delved into our own histories and that of "the other," we are ready to consider Lapsley's challenging second and third acknowledgment questions. Please be sure to read the caveats below.

1. What did I/we do to others?
2. What did I/we fail to do?

Caveats: The timing of when these questions are asked is critical. There are some situations for which they are inappropriate, for example, in cases of child or domestic abuse. However, survivors on a healing journey to recover from childhood trauma may find them useful in examining the choices they are making *as adults* in how they are responding. And individuals and groups who suffered unjustified attacks

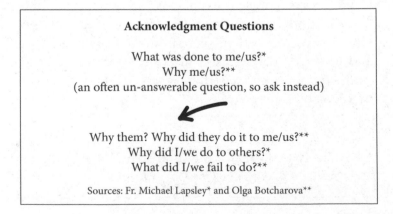

Acknowledgment Questions

What was done to me/us?*
Why me/us?**
(an often un-answerable question, so ask instead)

Why them? Why did they do it to me/us?**
Why did I/we do to others?*
What did I/we fail to do?**

Sources: Fr. Michael Lapsley* and Olga Botcharova**

or structural injustice may find them useful in looking at how unaddressed trauma has entrapped them
in acting in or acting out cycles of violence.[49]

Facing history opens our eyes to the wider context of a current event and to the complexity of life.
It makes us aware that who is named "victim" or
"aggressor" depends upon the segment of history we
are looking at and from whose side we are viewing
the story. It leads to the ability to openly acknowledge hypocrisy and own transgressions and those of
our people.[50]

Anna shares from her story:

*I said to myself, "Anna, you are really angry." It was
cellular, a physical, raw rage. And then I realized
this is the same rage, the same level where the guys
ran the planes into the building—helpless, desperate
to make a change in conditions. Wow! I knew I had
to engage this post 9/11 journey until it was done.
I really needed to understand as much as I could
about the nuts and bolts about what created this
situation and what was so painful for other people
that this was the best they could do to express their
needs. And I'm still not done.*

Reflecting on Lapsley's questions, then, opens a space
within us to see our own shadows, our own shortcomings, our own failings. We can face and acknowledge all our story, the good and the painful aspects—
the valor, heroism, sacrifice, pain, fear, resilience,
betrayals, humiliations, shortcomings, atrocities, and
guilty secrets we may have withheld. The process
brings us face-to-face with our own prejudices and
biases. It begins the process of rehumanizing the

demonized enemy. And it shatters simplistic, scape-goating, polarizing, good-versus-evil narratives that perpetuate cycles of violence, opening us to new and liberating stories.

This process of seeing both ourselves and "the other" from a more complex perspective can take months or even years. It represents a major shift in identity and happens best when some degree of psychological safety is assured. As we learn more about "the other," our anger and hatred begin to be replaced by understanding and even compassion, a sense of affinity and humility.[51] The body/brain can shed shame and humiliation and reenactment behaviors can cease. The transgenerational effects of trauma can end, releasing future generations from its burden.

Nicaraguan psychologist Martha Cabrera observes that when people who have lived through trauma began to reconstruct, talk about, reflect on, and accept their personal and national history, a fundamental change occurred. Despite all their suffering, they found meaning and significance in what they had lived through, and in what they had now become. This process helped them move forward in positive ways.[52]

Acknowledgement is a powerful process. Think of times someone has recognized your point of view, your suffering, the injustice against your people. Acknowledging your own and "the other's" story requires vulnerability and courage. What a gift to ourselves and others! Acknowledgment moves healing forward, preparing us to take risks with action and policy unimaginable only a short time before. It is spiritual work of the deepest sort and can be truly transformational.[53]

Facing the past, the reality of the present, and the challenges in the future open the way for post-traumatic growth.

Reconnection: *Recognizing interdependence, taking risks (#6–#8)*

With an understanding of history comes a consciousness of our fundamental interconnectedness and interdependence as people, cultures, and nations. This awareness may lead to openness to risk contact with the other. A commitment to risk is not an injunction to put oneself in harm's way or to be in an abusive situation.[54] Individuals, communities, or nations must decide what level of risk they are ready to take, and no one should be coerced. When former enemies meet, strong emotions can be re-triggered as old memories and emotions come flooding back. Individuals and communities should be equipped with an array of brain/body self-regulating tools that they use before, during, and after encounters. Trained support people may also be an asset.

Trauma researcher Bessel van der Kolk says that although studies have not been conducted with conflicted groups, if he were to guess what brain/body tools might help them engage constructively, he would suggest practices such as qigong and yoga.[55] Observe what healthy practices people in your context already use to self-regulate and relax and incorporate them as you address trauma. Patricia Mathes Cane teaches exercises that elicit the relaxation response gleaned from various parts of the world to villagers, professionals, political prisoners, health workers, and community groups in many places of trauma and conflict.[56] These workouts help brain function to become, and remain, integrated, even in the midst of challenging encounters.

How engagement with "the other" takes place will vary with the situation. When the harm has been personal, one-on-one meetings can take place either alone (if there is adequate safety), or with a third-party facilitator. In some cultures, exchanges take place through intermediaries or through community processes.

At a social level, the Truth and Reconciliation Commissions provide a way for some victims to tell their "truths" and to find answers and hear apologies in a public forum. In South Africa, victims were also able to listen to the testimony of perpetrators. Although only a few cases allowed for direct encounter between the two sides, the hearings often did address important needs and served to humanize "the other."

Ordinary citizens do not have to wait for official peace treaties to be signed to meet the other side in situations of conflict. Programs such as Seeds of Peace[57] bring young people from both sides of a conflict together in camp and home settings. A mountain retreat in Caux, Switzerland, has provided an unofficial meeting place for adversaries since World War II. In Sudan, a sewing class was formed for women on opposite sides of the conflict. In the United States, the organization Coming to the Table brings together descendants of those who were enslaved and those who enslaved them to address the unresolved and persistent effects of the institution of slavery.[58]

Sometimes, meeting the offender is impossible. After 9/11, the hijackers of the planes were dead, and meeting with other Al Qaeda members was not an option. So, a number of people who had lost family members formed the organization "September 11th Families for Peaceful Tomorrows." Some traveled to Afghanistan or Iraq to share stories and grieve with civilians there who had lost family members in the "war on terror." With a goal of turning grief into peace, they continue as an advocacy group, promoting policies of nonviolence, understanding, and engagement to break cycles of violence.[59]

When neighbors have caused harm, it can be especially difficult to go beyond a surface level of understanding to reach a place of security and safety. This long process is aided by discovering each other's history, by getting outside help, and by gaining an understanding of how individual and collective memory is shaped by facts, perception, and neuroception. The Sierra Leonean organization Fambul Tok (Family Talk) has created community-owned processes to promote healing and reconciliation among neighbors-turned-enemies during a civil war.[60]

The conflict transformation process of meeting together is not to use suffering as a weapon against each other, but to increase understanding and compassion.[61,62] As we have seen, when we choose to act in new ways, the brain literally forms new neural pathways. Healthy encounters contradict the helplessness and paralysis of the traumatizing events. They contradict the habitual way of responding to stressful triggers that further weaken feelings of control and

> When we choose to act in new ways, the brain forms new neural pathways.

connection.[63] Something powerful happens when we meet face-to-face. That something powerful shows up physiologically. Stephan Porges found that positive social engagement calms the nervous system, helping it move out of mobilization fight-flight.[64,65]

> In meeting each other, we discover that we're really part of the same family that somehow has got broken up.
> —Rev. Kenneth Newell, Northern Ireland[66]

Encounters with "the other" can lead to a shared sense of responsibility to reshape the future and restore harmony at all levels. Creative ideas flow, we feel more resilient, and others are drawn to the process. We discover the revolutionary paradox that we become more secure when we promote the security of each other, friend and foe alike. Emotions which used to pull us down begin to raise us up,[67] powering individual and collective efforts to transform the social landscape and meet needs for safety and justice.

Lam observes:

Yes, there are still rebels in the bush, and the area is still insecure. They just ambushed one of our priests, and three people died. They just chopped off the fingers of a woman. But some came out of the bush . . . and they are being integrated back into the community. Those rebels, they are our former enemy. But I am meeting with their leaders and helping them with income-generation projects and organization and bookkeeping. One day the chairman of the group came to me and said, "I hear you are doing workshops for the community on peace. Don't you think we need a workshop on peace?" So I will do a workshop for them. We will focus on human relationships. It will help their reintegration process.

Reconnection: *Choosing whether to forgive (#9)*

To some, forgiving is an obscene word in the wake of profound human wrongdoing and evil. Indeed, the effort to forgive will seem like a burden and do more harm than good if it is

> Forgiveness is NOT forgetting or forgoing justice.

defined as forgetting, equated with forgoing the quest for justice, or experienced as a moral or religious duty rather than a hopeful possibility.

Forgiving is especially difficult when violence is ongoing or if harm has not been acknowledged. But when one has witnessed or experienced the bitterness that can consume individuals and groups as they spin in cycles of victimhood and violence, it is evident that humans need a loftier goal than punishment or revenge, even in the face of great suffering.[68]

Forgiving offers a release from the poison of bitterness. It does not mean giving up the quest for justice, but rather letting go of the cycles of revenge and retribution in order to pursue a justice that is restorative to victims and aggressors alike—a justice that may lay the groundwork for reconciliation.

Forgiving is made easier if our hurt has been acknowledged by others, especially by "the other," the aggressor or "enemy." Yet, if we make our forgiveness conditional—waiting to forgive until those who hurt us take steps toward reconciliation—we stay forever in their power. Regardless of *their* actions or responses, *we* choose whether to walk the journey of forgiveness.

Forgiving takes on new meaning if we have done the hard work of both parts of acknowledgment, rehumanizing "the other" by acknowledging their story (#5). As we have seen, the

> ## Humans need a loftier goal than punishment or revenge.

designation of "victim" and "aggressor" often depends on the particular segment of history we are viewing. Therefore, reciprocal acts of acknowledgment, remorse, repentance, and forgiveness are appropriate in many cases. For example, religious leaders in both Britain and Ireland have expressed remorse and asked each other for forgiveness for their part in the conflict.[69]

> True forgiveness is achieved in community. . . . It is history working itself out as grace, and it can be accomplished only in truth. That truth, however, is not mere knowledge. It is acknowledgment. It is a coming to terms with and it is a labor.
> —Hannah Arendt[70]

In forgiving, the intrapersonal, interpersonal, and collective are intertwined in complex ways. Ethics scholar Donald Shriver describes forgiveness in a political context as "an act that joins moral truth, forbearance, empathy, and commitment to repair a fractured human relationship."[71]

The Woodstock Center of Georgetown University held a series of meetings to explore how forgiveness is operationalized at national levels. The participants agreed that a culture of forgiveness must be built through actions at the personal, cultural, and political levels. National and civil society leaders in positions of sym-

> If we make our forgiveness conditional— waiting to forgive until those who hurt us take steps toward reconciliation—we stay forever in their power.

bolic authority play a critical role in moving the society in a direction of forgiveness and creating openness for creative reconciliation later.[72] We can learn much about forgiveness from countries like Rwanda or Sierra Leone, where survivors and perpetrators of the genocide often live close to one another. With nowhere else to go, they must find a way forward, and various degrees of forgiveness have been part of the process.[73,74]

Forgiving also may involve restitution. As we become aware of how we have wronged others, we recognize our need to take responsibility to repair as much as we can through payments or acts of service that in some way seek to balance the score. This can be both an individual and collective responsibility. Collective responsibility does not need to be done at a national level, nor does it need to be sponsored by the state. In recent years, universities in the United States have started telling the truth about the role of enslaved people in building their institutions. Some have established scholarship funds to make reparations. We can all find ways to live into a future that will be different from the past.

Reconnection: *Seeking justice (#10 #11)*

In a perfect world, justice would begin with the offenders—whether individuals, groups, or governments—admitting guilt, apologizing publicly, offering compensation, and making sure that the events do not happen again.

But the world is not perfect. Neither is justice. Nor are victims' expectations always clear or realistic. Often, people have an unspoken assumption that justice will restore a sense of normalcy and relieve the pain. It may to some degree, but often it cannot and does not. Sometimes justice can satisfy an abstract sense of what is right but it often fails to help those who have been harmed to break out of the cycles of victimhood or violence. In fact, as poet and playwright Bertolt Brecht reportedly said, "The fight for justice can make people ugly. That is, your motive in fighting for justice can be as ugly as the thing that you're seeking to fight."[75]

This does not mean that individuals and groups should not seek justice. Rather, it is an acknowledgment that the needs that trauma and violence create are complex, and that there are limits to the healing the justice system alone can provide.

The usual approach to justice in today's world is the legal or criminal justice approach, enshrined in national systems as well as international tribunals. Ideally, justice serves the common good and helps to create order. This justice approach tends to be organized around three questions:

1. What law was broken?
2. Who did it?
3. What do they deserve?

What they are seen to deserve, usually, is some form of punishment.

At its best, the legal justice system is designed to safeguard human rights and provide an orderly justice process. It often plays a vital role in identifying wrongdoers and denouncing wrongdoing.

Transitional justice is a way of assisting societies that have endured repressive rule or armed conflict to find ways that hold those responsible for past mass atrocities or human rights abuses accountable. Transitional justice may include judicial and nonjudicial responses such as prosecuting individual perpetrators, paying reparations to victims of state-sponsored violence, establishing truth-seeking initiatives about past abuse, and supporting reforming institutions like the police and the courts.

Sincere attempts at justice, however, can fall short. Aggressors may never be caught or may be unavailable. Courts, tribunals, and truth commissions are costly and cannot satisfy or even hear all who deserve to be heard. Legal systems can be corrupt; racial or ethnic bias can be present. If the damage was caused by organized crime or by a government, impunity may rule the day. The legal system also is limited in its ability to address the needs of those who have been harmed or aid in healing. Preoccupied with making sure wrongdoers get what they deserve, it does little to encourage offenders to understand what they did or to take real responsibility for their actions. In addition, its often-adversarial style exacerbates conflicts and wounds more than it heals. To pin one's hopes on the legal system bringing healing is often unrealistic.

Given these limitations, many people worldwide are reawakening to the principles and practices of restorative justice. Restorative justice focuses on harms that have been done and offers an understanding of justice that attends to the needs and obligations of those who have been harmed. Restorative justice can be used outside of or in tandem with the legal system, making it an empowering tool for communities and a hopeful way forward.[76]

Restorative justice is based on practices originating in indigenous and traditional societies and is organized around the following questions:

- Who has been harmed?
- What are their needs?
- Whose obligation is it to meet those needs?
- What are the causes of the harm?
- Who has a stake in the situation?
- What process can involve all in addressing needs and obligations and finding a solution?

The question "Who has been harmed?" acknowledges that those victimized must be central to the process, and that harm ripples out beyond direct victims. Family, friends, the community, and society as a whole may have been hurt. The offender, too, may be among those who have been hurt: for example, the offender may have been abused in the past, demonstrating again the complexity of the labels of "victim" and "offender."

Key concepts of restorative justice:

- Harm and needs
- Obligations/responsibility
- Engagement

Restorative justice also focuses on accountability. Those who caused the harm must face and acknowledge the hurt their actions created and take responsibility to right those wrongs as much as possible. It seeks to involve those who have been impacted by the wrongdoing in the solution. In some circumstances, it may involve a facilitated meeting between victims and offenders, but only at the request of the victim.

Healing justice approaches:

- Restorative justice
- Transformative justice
- Creative justice

When the act(s) of harm, even in part, resulted from unhealthy relationships, or social or political structures, the search for justice requires that we look not only at individual acts, but at collective responsibility and systemic causes. *Transformative justice* asks:

- What circumstances and structures permitted or encouraged this injury?
- What structural similarities exist between this and other similar acts or incidents?

- What measures can be taken to change these structures and circumstances to reduce future occurrences?

Transformative justice can be used by communities when the State fails to provide justice for individuals or groups. For example, in the United States, people of color sometimes hesitate to turn to the police or courts because of documented inequities in the system. Transformative justice is seen as having the potential for communities to provide safety to victims and accountability for harm-doers, to reduce violence, heal past trauma, and move the community toward equity and liberation.[77]

GenerationFIVE, a volunteer collaborative organization in several US cities, is a case in point. They recognized that while child sexual abuse rates are high, it is rarely reported. When it is reported, retribution and punishment result, but not justice, safety, or transformed relationships and communities. Root causes contributing to the problem, such as gender inequality, class exploitation, racism, violence, and threat of difference are not addressed. Using a community-based transformative justice approach, their goal is to end child abuse in five generations.[78]

The concepts of restorative justice and transformative justice are embedded in Canadian Gwawaenuk Chief Dr. Robert Joseph's writing on reconciliatory justice, which is being used to address and settle land seizure and other injustices against indigenous peoples. Joseph describes reconciliatory justice as "a dispute resolution concept, ideal, process, for overcoming the politics of denial and for appropriately resolving . . . post-settlement challenges, issues, and tensions."[79]

Another proactive route to doing justice is what Wilma Derksen calls creative justice: creating a symbolic act or project that counters the darkness of what was done and/or works to prevent that harm from happening again. For example, since Wilma and Cliff Derksen's daughter, Candace, was murdered in Winnipeg, Canada in 1984, Wilma has become a victim-and-justice reform advocate, writing, speaking, organizing dialogues between victims and inmates, and more.[80] The September 11th Families for Peaceful Tomorrows will not have their day in court, but they have formed relationships with people affected by violence across the globe and focus on creating a world where hate and revenge does not have the final word.[81] Torture survivors formed the Torture Abolition and Survivors Support Coalition International (TASSC) to provide psychological support to survivors, putting their energy into ending torture through advocacy and educating policymakers.[82]

The work of seeking formal justice can continue simultaneously with creative justice initiatives. But one's energy, future, and gifts are not held hostage to traumatic injustice or the outcome in a legal ruling.

Ideally, then, justice addresses the past and sets things as right as is possible, so that we can move into the future. It may open the way for joint planning with former adversaries to initiate projects such as writing a common history together so that the "us versus them" story is more nuanced and multilayered (#11). A primary goal becomes assuring human security and dignity for all. This is possible if both sides can answer the question "What would make a culture and a system that meets the deepest needs of your opponents?"[83]

> **The paradox of security** is that I/we become more secure when we promote the security of our neighbors, even the "other." Real security rests on the promotion of just and peaceful relationships among individuals, groups, and nations. It allows us to feel safe and function from the social engagement system and connecting brain rather than the defensiveness of fight/flight.

Reconnection: *Possibility of reconciliation* (#12)

Reconciliation is not an event that happens at a precise moment. It evolves slowly from the labor and grace of the healing journey. Achieving "as much justice as possible"[84] and forgiving are key elements, but they do not guarantee reconciliation. When reconciliation happens, it is evident in relationships. Attitudes, beliefs, and behaviors toward former opponents, enemies, and offenders are transformed. Cooperation replaces polarization. Trauma and suffering are neither forgotten nor excused, but better understood and integrated into a new self or group identity (#12). A sense of efficacy and well-being replaces fear.

Anna says:

> *This doesn't go away; it's not over. In a sense, this is a beginning; I can almost honestly say the word "gift." This is an existential, full-on call from the deepest depths of what we call God to really get real about what is important, what is truth, what is life about, not just in an understanding way, but in a way that changes how I live and demands an impeccable and lifelong commitment.*

Something transcendent happens as individuals and groups choose to address trauma. We don't have to "effort" ourselves into resilience. We discover that just as trauma and violence are linked, so are trauma healing and resilience. We surprise ourselves with our strength and capacity for growth. We feel the energy of being a part of the healing of our world. Cycles of life replace cycles of violence. We realize we are more than we ever knew.

> Just as trauma and violence are linked, so are trauma healing and resilience.

The last two chapters are about implementation. Chapter 6 imagines *what if* some of these principles had been part of the US response to 9/11. Chapter 7 suggests ways to apply what you've learned to yourself and your community right now.

6.
9/11 and Breaking the Cycles, 2005 and 2019:
Applying STAR

"The role of the peacebuilder is to interrupt the transmission of woundedness."

—James O'Dea[1]

When I was little, my sisters and I played "house" with our dolls as our children; we made up families and a running verbal narrative. The storyline would flow with one of us picking up where the other left off as we acted out the imagined events. Occasionally, the tale spun off in a direction we didn't like. So, one of us would simply say, "Let's erase that." Sometimes we paused momentarily for a bit of negotiation. But usually, without missing a beat, the narrator simply returned to an earlier junction of the story, and we played out a different ending.

If only real life were so simple. Alas, the magic of "erase that" belongs to childhood. Lacking easy solutions, we can fall into griping, regret, and a plethora of "what if" questions that keep us stuck in the past. But "what if" can also be used to imagine a different future—and even a different present. In the 2005 edition of this book, I wrote:

> So, let's go back to September 11, 2001 and imagine—what if?
>
> *What if* in the awful days after 9/11, our US leaders—the president and our governors, mayors, clergy, and health professionals—had normalized our feelings of anger, bewilderment, humiliation, horror, and our desire for justice and vindication as common trauma reactions? *What if* they had stated clearly that, although these low-mode reactions are normal, they should not determine our response?
>
> *What if* our leaders had known that their own trauma reactions to an attack happening on their watch could affect their judgment? *What if* they had displayed a greatness born of humility by asking our allies to help formulate a response?
>
> *What if* those heinous acts had been named a crime rather than an act of war? *What if* the US had then asked a sympathetic international community for cooperation and help in dismantling terrorist networks, bringing them to justice, and interrupting the financial support systems that feed them?[2]
>
> *What if* we had been encouraged to reach out to our Muslim or immigrant neighbors with

random acts of kindness? *What if* cities and towns had encouraged citizens to channel their trauma energy into organized hikes, dances, soccer games, tennis and golf tournaments, walks, races, and car washes to raise money for the victims and survivors of violence worldwide?

What if national days of mourning had been called for the purpose of being silent together, to meditate, to pray, so that we could listen for guidance and wisdom to discern a nonconventional response to the nonconventional act of flying planes into buildings?[3] *What if* the rest of the world had been invited to join us?

What if, in response to the question "Why do they hate us?", our government had invited universities, journalists, television networks, filmmakers, and artists to produce programs to help us understand the relevant history? *What if* they had interviewed ordinary people and leaders from the Middle East and elsewhere about what their life is like on a day-to-day basis? What if they had been asked to tell us how their lives have been impacted, positively and negatively, by the US, and asked to tell us what they thought led to 9/11?

What if in the study and exploration of root causes, we had discovered that for a long time, real people around the globe had not only benefited from the generosity of the US, but had also been harmed—and even killed—because of our policies? What if such a discovery had allowed us to reject good-versus-evil narratives and redemptive violence solutions as simplistic and dangerous?

What if, with the encouragement and support of our leaders, average citizens—including the 82 percent of US citizens who have never traveled abroad—participated in exchange visits, work camps, and seminars to learn together about how the lives of US citizens are intertwined with the lives of citizens in the rest of the world?

What if we had said to each other, "We're sorry. Never again should policies or acts of terror happen—to you, to us, to anyone else."

What if even a fraction of the money spent on the war on terror was used to pay for health care, schools, and job training in the US and around the globe?

What if war doesn't stop terrorism?

What if it's not too late to take steps in another direction?

Now, as I write, it is 2019. Hundreds of thousands of civilians and military personnel have lost their lives in the "endless wars" in Afghanistan and the Middle East. Trillions of dollars have been spent, dollars put on a "national credit card" on which the US is currently only paying the interest because the wars were not funded by new taxes or war bonds.[4]

But security still eludes us. Global terrorism attacks have skyrocketed since 9/11.[5] There are more Taliban in Afghanistan today than in 2001.[6] A task force on extremism commissioned by the US Congress reported in 2018 that "despite our best efforts since 9/11 to counter terrorism and protect the homeland, the threat of extremism and its danger to the US has evolved, and it continues to grow."[7] It recommends a new approach aimed at prevention.

War exacerbates the climate crisis. Between 2010 and 2015, the operations of the Department of Defense, the world's largest single user of oil and other petroleum products, added an average of 44 million metric tons of CO_2 per year to the atmosphere. According to the Costs of War Project at Brown University, "Spending on war and fuel use will only diminish the capacity of the US to develop resiliency and reduce green-house gas emissions."[8]

The horror of war makes its way home in the form of almost a million US veterans living with long-term physical disabilities and many more living with the effects of trauma. Veterans are killing themselves at an average rate of 20 per day and the suicide rate among active-duty military members is alarming.[9] For every soldier deployed, there is a family deprived of stability. For every veteran, there is a family that bears the secondary traumas of the war.

What if conventional security doesn't always make us safer?

What if war doesn't stop terrorism?

What if it's not too late to take steps in another direction?

7.
How Then Shall We Live?

"Humankind has not woven the web of life.
We are but one thread within it.
Whatever we do to the web, we do to ourselves.
All things are bound together. All things connect."
— *Chief Seattle, Leader of the Suquamish and*
Duwamish Native American tribes

I have yet to meet a person or group that doesn't want to leave a better world for their children, grandchildren, and great-grandchildren. Yet how that longing is carried out can be healing—or destructive. Here are seven suggestions for living in ways that transmit intergenerational legacies of healing and resilience rather than trauma and violence.

1. Gain new perspectives by applying the STAR model in everyday life.
The news every day provides ample case examples of the three-part STAR model: (a) the trauma

experience; (b) cycles of violence against ourselves or others due to unaddressed trauma; and (c) the process of breaking cycles of violence and building resilience. Try viewing the news through the lens of this model. For example:

- As you listen to a headline story, ask who is/ are the identified victim(s)? The identified aggressor(s)? Might the roles be different if we were looking at another segment of their history?
- Notice the narratives promoted by leaders, the media, and ordinary people—maybe even you: us versus them; good versus evil; redemptive violence; chosen trauma. Are you witnessing the trance-like "rituals of large-group psychology" (see Chapter 4) being played out?
- Notice examples of healing, resilience, and acting well in spite of threat by individuals and groups. Celebrate the ripple effects!

One of the everyday ways many of us unwittingly contribute to othering and good-versus-evil thinking is by the casual use of the terms "good guys" and "bad guys." These oversimplified phrases remove "bad" from ourselves, our group, or our country. They reduce a complex human being to a single descriptor. They allow us to ignore our own shadow side while projecting harm and evil onto others. Even young children can be taught the difference between bad choices and behavior and being a "bad guy."

2. Speak up against violence: silence gives consent.
Ervin Staub, PhD, has devoted his life to researching the psychology of good and evil, the roots of mass violence and genocide, and why we as humans help or harm others. He says it's up to us, we the people, to speak out early on against us-versus-them rhetoric and actions, pointedly questioning those who perpetrate hate.[1]

When we don't get involved because we don't want to "be political," or because we think we won't make a difference, aggressors are emboldened, taking our silence as approval. Being a passive bystander is not neutrality and can have deadly consequences. Staub says our repose, or lack thereof, largely determines whether the flames of hate are extinguished, or the situation escalates into violence.[2] Our voices matter.

> I imagine one of the reasons people cling to their hate so stubbornly is because they sense, once hate is gone, they will be forced to deal with pain.
> —James Baldwin, Writer, Activist, Playwright

Violence prevention researcher Joseph Bock calls specifically on people of faith to challenge those within their own religious traditions who preach hate or use scripture to sanction atrocities, bigotry, and aggression.[3] It's a criminal offense to deliberately spread Ebola, polio, or measles. Is it also criminal to keep people so focused on threat and othering that they find it difficult to feel safe, dimming the ability to be reflective, modulate fear, and connect?

101

In the midst of divisiveness and violence, it's easy to forget that hurt people hurt people. It's a challenge to confront a hate-spewing individual or group with one hand, while holding in our other hand, awareness and compassion for the wound and pain beneath the hate.

3. Develop a toolkit of trauma release exercises and body/brain calming practices.
In a turbulent world, enhance your resilience by learning two types of tools: (a) trauma release exercises that discharge the energy of fight/flight and help prevent post-traumatic reactions; and (b) body/brain self- and co-regulating practices that calm us so we can act with clarity, compassion, and courage in the midst of stress rather than being instinct-driven and fearfully reactive. Review Chapter 5 for tools that can be used individually or in groups by anyone, not just psychologists.

These simple but powerful practices can be used as emotional first aid tools in times of crisis, for mitigating everyday stresses, and for helping us live well together and engage in civil discourse. Imagine the effects on a community or society if they were widely promoted and practiced in the challenging hours, weeks, months, and years after natural disasters, school shootings, or political bombshells. Envision incorporating them in town hall meetings when divisive issues are on the agenda, during contentious legal cases, in restorative justice processes, anti-racism work, or post-conflict negotiations. The purpose is not to shut down anger or stifle objections, but to recognize when discussions are going "down the ladder" and help us co-regulate back into our social engagement systems. Instead of demonizing each other and fanning fear, we have a better chance of addressing the issues at hand with flexibility, creativity, and "intuitive ways of knowing that fuel wisdom."[4]

4. Work for change of hearts AND structures/systems.

Effective justice and conflict transformation work that reduces traumagenic events requires attention to both personal transformation and structural change. Countless revolutions have overthrown corrupt, oppressive regimes, only to turn out as bad or worse because the hearts of the new leaders were no different than those they replaced. Anger can be the spark plug of a movement but love from an awakened heart must be the sustaining energy. Otherwise, the way we work for change adds to the hatred, othering, cruelty, and fear of the world.

Changing hearts one person at a time is important, but it not enough. Insisting it is *the* way to work for lasting change ignores both the reality of systems and the millions of people suffering from injustice and evil who need help and structural change now. Imagine being a refugee cradling your starving child in a barren camp, and someone tells you that assistance will come only when the hearts of the leaders soften. How much would you care about personal change?

Martin Luther King Jr. said, "The law cannot make a man love me, but it can stop him from lynching me." Work to change structures *and* hearts, starting with your own. Both are essential as long as we're fallible human beings living in a complex world.

5. Discover the power and possibilities of nonviolence.

As we saw in Chapter 5, the use, and success, of nonviolent civil resistance campaigns has increased over the last century, while the success rate of violent campaigns has declined.[5] Ordinary citizens play a pivotal role in nonviolent movements.

What if we studied nonviolence with the same intensity that we now study how to wage war? Form a nonviolence study group or take an online class (see resource list on page 130). Get acquainted with the scores of tactics that can be done on the street or in one's living room, from strikes to marches, mock funerals, humorous skits, walkouts, and letter writing/social media campaigns.[6] Choose what fits your values, your interests, and your sphere of influence. Pay attention to your own heart and spirit: nonviolence is not only about turning away from external violence, but also letting go of the internal violence we may harbor in our spirits. *How* you show up matters.

Then counter the paralysis of discouragement, despair, and trauma by getting involved. You join a long tradition that includes famous names like Martin Luther King Jr., Dorothy Day, and Abdul Ghaffar Khan, the Pakistani contemporary of Gandhi, whose army of nonviolent Pashtun warriors suffered greatly as they stood against British rule. You join thousands of ordinary citizens all over the world who eschew violence as a means to an end.

6. Stay informed of the news—and find the news that doesn't make the news.

In an era of cyberattacks, spin, and fake news, being informed can feel like a fraught journey through landmines and quicksand. Counter media news silos by accessing a variety of domestic and international sources, available with a click of a mouse. Take occasional breaks if you feel overwhelmed by the barrage of disasters, wrangling, and hate. The threats and challenges in our world can be frightening, maddening, and even traumagenic to the point of paralysis.

Counter despair by finding the news and people beneath the news: initiatives that are percolating around the world that rarely make the headlines. Join concerned citizens in your community working to heal trauma, prevent violence, build bridges across divisions, dismantle discrimination, and create just, local economies. Join those who steadily persist in advocating for sane climate crisis policy even in the face of corporations and politicians who lack the will to lead in ways that could prevent disaster. Appreciate your neighbors, cherish children, hug your friends. Leadership and organizational behavior expert Margaret Wheatley says that in uncertain times, we can find joy by using our power, influence, insight, and compassion to create "islands of sanity" locally.[7] She is describing a way of co-regulating and acting well in the face of threat.

If your house is burning with your children inside, no one talks about political affiliation, religion, race, class, sexual orientation, ableism, or gender. We all just want everyone to be safe. Is there a point in chaotic times when the balance tips from hate and othering to realizing we're all in the same boat, part of the same web of life? To wanting security for all, friend and foe alike which makes us all safer? If so, we then transmit strong legacies of healing and resilience to our children and grandchildren.

7. Remember that we are not alone.
Addressing trauma, preventing or breaking cycles of violence, and transforming relationships is life-long work we can't do alone. Pray. Meditate. Tune in to the wisdom of body, heart, mind, and spirit. In the company of each other, find sustenance for the journey from the Source of Life who has promised that light overcomes darkness, and that a peace beyond our fears animates and guides when we say yes to addressing trauma in life-affirming ways.

Endnotes

Preface

1. Olga Butcharova, "Implementation of Track Two Diplomacy" in *Forgiveness and Reconciliation*, eds. Raymond G. Helmick and Rodney L. Petersen (Radnor, PA: Templeton Foundation Press, 2001).
2. Lisa Schirch, *The Little Book of Strategic Peacebuilding: A Vision and Framework for Peace With Justice* (Intercourse, PA: Good Books, 2004), 9.
3. David Anderson Hooker and Amy Czajkowski, Transforming Historical Harms, Eastern Mennonite University, Center for Justice and Peacebuilding, Accessed February 6, 2020. https://emu.edu/cjp/docs/transforming-historical-harms.pdf.
4. Ibid.
5. The "Wozo" (resilience) program in Haiti is a long-term contextualized country-wide response to the 2010 earthquake that under the leadership of Garly Michel, Harry Thelusma, Adley Dumay, and Lydie Mia Legitime-Vil established a network of trained persons that continues to help individuals, families, and communities. Everett M. Ressler, "Evaluation of the Trauma Healing Program "Twomatizasyon ak Wozo" STAR Haiti

Programme." Unpublished paper, The Konterra Group, June 17, 2013.

6. Judah Oudshoorn, Michelle Jackett, and Lorraine Stutzman, *The Little Book of Restorative Justice for Sexual Abuse: Hope through Trauma* (New York: Good Books, 2015).

7. Coming to the Table (CTTT), www.comingto thetable.org, brings together descendants of slave-owning families and descendants of those they enslaved and uses the STAR framework. Will Hairston, a descendent of one of the largest slave-owning families in the Old South, worked with the Center for Justice and Peacebuilding to seek funding and develop the initiative. See Tom DeWolf and Jodie Geddes, *The Little Book of Racial Healing: Coming to the Table for Truth-Telling, Liberation, and Transformation* (New York: Good Books, 2019).

8. Green String Network does trauma-informed peacebuilding work using an adaptation of the STAR model in East Africa incorporating folktales, case studies, and artwork. www.green-string.org.

Chapter 1: Introduction

1. *International Cooperation at a Crossroads: Aid, trade and security in an unequal world*, United Nations Development Program, February 2020. http://hdr.undp.org/sites/default/files/hdr_2005 _summary_en.pdf.

2. Bessel A. van der Kolk, *The Body Keeps the Score: Brain, Mind, and Body in the Health of Trauma* (New York: Viking Penguin Group, 2014), 347–356.

3. John Gottman, *Why Marriages Succeed or Fail* (New York: Simon and Schuster, 1994),176–177.

Chapter 2: Definition, Sources, and Types of Trauma

1. Carolyn Yoder, Skype Interview with Lam Cosmos, July 2004.
2. Jeff Goodell, "How Climate Change and Wall Street Almost Killed Puerto Rico," *Rolling Stone*, September 12, 2018. https://www.rollingstone .com/politics/politics-features/puerto-rico -hurricane-maria-damage-722570.
3. Todd Beer, "Police Killing of Blacks: Data for 2015, 2016, 2017, and first half of 2018." The Society Pages, Sociology Toolbox, March 1, 2018. Updated August 24, 2018. https://thesocietypages. org/toolbox/police-killing-of-blacks.
4. Katie Arnold, "Why I Fled: Twelve stories of lost homes, lost lives, and the perilous search for safety, CNN.com, August 2017. https://www .cnn.com/interactive/2017/09/world/myanmar -rohingya-refugee-stories.
5. Canadian TV News Staff, "Residential School Survivors Share Their Stories." June 2, 2015. https: //www.ctvnews.ca/canada/residential-school- survivors-share- their-stories-1.2403561,
6. Justine Masika Bihamba, "The 'rape capital of the world'? We women in Congo don't see it that way." The Guardian, October 9, 2017. https: //www.theguardian.com/global-development /2017/oct/09/the-rape-capital-of-the-world-we -women-in-democratic-republic-congo-dont-see-it -that-way.
7. Numerous studies show women have higher rates of Post-Traumatic Stress Disorder than men. I do not include gender as a factor here, however, because I believe men may exhibit symptoms of

trauma differently than women, and if a wider range of explanatory variables (such as anger, substance abuse, difficulty with intimacy) were considered, the rates may be similar.

8. David Anderson Hooker and Amy Czajkowski, *Transforming Historical Harms*, Eastern Mennonite University, Center for Justice and Peacebuilding, Accessed February 6, 2020. https://emu.edu/cjp /docs/transforming-historical-harms.pdf.

9. D. Summerfield, "Addressing Human Response to War and Atrocity," in *Beyond Trauma: Cultural and Societal Dynamics*, eds. Rolf J. Kebler, Charles R. Figley, and Berthold R.R. Gersons (New York: Plenum Press, 1995), 22.

10. Martha Cabrera-Cruz, "Living and Surviving in a Multiply Wounded Country," Universität Klagenfurt, Accessed February 6, 2020. http: //www.uni-klu.ac.at/ ~ hstockha/neu/html/cabre racruz.htm.

11. Pat Vivian and Shana Hormann, Organizational Trauma and Healing (CreateSpace Independent Publishing Platform, 2013). http://organizational traumaandhealing.com/what-is-organizational -trauma.

12. "Shared Trauma: Helping Clients Cope with National Events That Affect the Therapist," American Psychological Association. Accessed March 31, 2019. https://www.apapracticecentral .org/ce/self-care/shared.

13. George Marshall, *Don't Even Think of It: Why Our Brains Are Wired to Ignore Climate Change* (Berryville, VA: Bloomsbury USA, 2014), 46–47.

14. Molly Castelloe, PhD, "Coming to Terms With Eco-anxiety: Growing an awareness of climate

change," January 9, 2018, Accessed July 30, 2019. https://www.psychologytoday.com/us/blog /the-me-in-we/201801/coming-terms-ecoanxiety.

15. Maria Yellow Horse Brave Heart, "The Historical Trauma Response Among Natives and Its Relationship with Substance Abuse: A Lakota Illustration," *Journal of Psychoactive Drugs* 35, no. 1 (2003): 7–13, doi:[10.1080/02791072.2003.1039 9988]. https://www.tandfonline.com/doi/abs/10.1 080/02791072.2003.10399988.

16. Nathaniel Vincent Mohatt et al. "Historical trauma as public narrative: A conceptual review of how history impacts present-day health," National Institutes of Health, January 21, 2014.

17. *Dawnland*, an Emmy award–winning documentary film addressing the historical and current harm of stolen children from the Wabanaki indigenous peoples in the United States, is an example of uncovering a "conspiracy of silence." *Dawnland*, directed by Adam Mazo and Ben Pender-Cudlip (Boston, MA.: Upstander Films, Inc., 2009) DVD, Blu-Ray, and Streaming. https://upstanderproject .org/dawnland

18. Rachel Yehuda and Linda M. Bierer, "The Relevance of Epigenetics to PTSD: Implications for the DSM-V," *Journal of Trauma Stress* 22, no. 5 (October 22, 2009): 427–434, doi: [10.1002/jts.20448], http://www.ncbi.nlm.nih.gov/pmc/articles /PMC2891396.

19. Philip de Barros, "The Ghost in Your Genes & The Science of Epigenetics," *Exploring Darwin 2016* (BBC Productions, 2016). https://vimeo.com /194100218.

20. Nagy A. Youssef et al., "The Effects of Trauma, with or without PTSD, on the Transgenerational DNA Methylation Alterations in Human Offsprings," *Brain Sci* 8, no. 5 (May 8, 2018): 83, doi: [10.3390/ brainsci8050083], https://www.ncbi.nlm.nih.gov /pmc/articles/PMC5977074.

21. A version of this article appears in print on Dec. 11, 2018, on Page D1 of the *New York Times* with the headline "Can We Inherit Trauma?" https://www. nytimes.com/2018/12/10/health/mind-epigenetics -genes.html?nytapp = true&smid = nytcore -ios-share&fbclid = IwAR1ShmcxOfi-NiwS6qB 8Gw6K0E2WcmDJ-Xf7V39ol5zMzckmdAkn _DUohv8.

22. At STAR, we use the term participation-induced traumatic stress and perpetration-induced traumatic stress depending on the situation. MacNair uses "perpetration." Rachael M. MacNair, *Perpetration -Induced Traumatic Stress: The Psychological Consequence of Killing* (Westport, CT: Praeger, 2002).

23. "What is Moral Injury?" The Moral Injury Project, Syracuse University. http://moralinjuryproject.syr .edu/about-moral-injury.

24. J. Shay Moral injury. Psychoanalytic Psychology 2014, 31(2), 182–191.

25. Grant H. Brenner, Considering Collective Moral Injury following the 2016 Election, Contemporary Psychoanalysis, doi: 10.1080/00107530.2017.1384683, https://www.psychologytoday.com/sites/default /files/considering_collective_moral_injury_following _the_2016_election.pdf.

26. William G. Cunningham, "Terrorism Definitions and Typologies" in *Terrorism: Concepts, Causes and Conflict Resolution* (George Mason University), 9.

http://www.au.af.mil/au/awc/awcgate/dtra/terror
ism_concepts.pdf.

27. Accidently harming or causing death to another
can be deeply traumagenic. See David Peters,
"What Happens to Your Life after You Accidently
Kill Someone." *The Guardian*, Nov. 29, 2018.
https://www.theguardian.com/global/2018
/nov/29/what-happens-to-your-life-after-you-acci
dentally-kill-someone.

28. Microaggressions are everyday verbal, nonverbal, and environmental slights, snubs, or insults,
whether intentional or unintentional, which
communicate hostile, derogatory, or negative
messages to target persons based solely upon
their marginalized group membership. David
Wing Sue, "Microaggressions: More Than Just
Race," *Psychology Today*, November 17, 2010.
https://www.psychologytoday.com/us/blog
/microaggressions-in-everyday-life/201011
/microaggressions-more-just-race.

29. Colorism is prejudice or discrimination against
individuals with a dark skin tone, typically among
people of the same ethnic or racial group. Lexico
Dictionary, Oxford. https://www.lexico.com/en/
definition/colorism.

**Chapter 3: The Trauma Experience: STAR
Model Part I**

1. For downloads of the three-part STAR model, go
to https://emu.edu/cjp/star/toolkit or www.Peace
AfterTrauma.com.

2. Stephen W. Porges, *The Pocket Guide to the Polyvagal
Theory: The Transformative Power of Feeling Safe*
(New York: W.W. Norton, 2017), 26–27.

3. Deb Dana, *The Polyvagal Theory in Therapy: Engaging the Rhythm of Regulation* (New York: W.W. Norton, 2018), 7–14.

4. Deb Dana, *Beginners Guide to Polyvagal Theory,* Rhythm of Regulation, Accessed February 2020. https://www.rhythmofregulation.com/resources /Beginner's%20Guide.pdf

5. Stephen W. Porges, *The Pocket Guide to the Polyvagal Theory,* 26–27.

6. Daniel J. Siegel, *Pocket Guide to Interpersonal Neurobiology: An Integrative Handbook of the Mind* (New York: W.W. Norton, 2012), 27-2 to 27-3.

7. Siegel, *Pocket Guide to Interpersonal Neurobiology,* 27-1 to 27-3.

8. Porges, *The Pocket Guide to the Polyvagal Theory,* 19.

9. Peter A. Levine, *Waking the Tiger: Healing Trauma* (Berkeley, CA: North Atlantic Books, 1997), 19–39.

10. This phrase was first used in 1949 by Donald Hebb, a Canadian neuropsychologist working in the field of associative learning. He hypothesized that if two neurons were active at the same time, the synapse between them would get stronger. In the early 1970s the first mechanism supporting Hebb's hypothesis was discovered. Exceptions have also been discovered. See "Neurons that fire together, don't always wire together: Neuroscientists uncover a new rule of connectivity of neurons in the neocortex," *Science News,* November 8, 2018. https://www .sciencedaily.com/releases/2018/11 /181108130537.htm which summarizes the findings of Mean-Hwan Kim et al., "Segregated Subnetworks of Intracortical Projection Neurons

in Primary Visual Cortex," *Neuron*, 2018; doi: 10.1016/j.neuron.2018.10.023

11. Levine, *Waking the Tiger*, 19–39.
12. Daniel J. Siegel and Mary Hartzell, *Parenting from the Inside Out: How a Deeper Self-Understanding Can Help You Raise Children Who Thrive* (New York City: Penguin, 2003), 174.
13. Ibid.
14. Howard Zehr, *Transcending: Reflections of Crime Victims* (Intercourse, PA: Good Books, 2001), 86–197.
15. Rolf J. Kleber, "Epilogue" in *Beyond Trauma: Cultural and Societal Dynamics*, eds. Rolf J. Kleber, Charles R. Figley, and Berthold P. R. Gersons (New York: Plenum Press, 1995), 302.
16. Judith Lewis Herman, *Trauma and Recovery* (New York: Basic Books, 1992), 158.
17. Cabrera-Cruz, https://www.medico.de/download /report26/ps_cabrera_en.pdfhttp://www.uni-klu .ac.at/~hstockha/neu/html/cabreracruz.htm.
18. Judy Barsalou, "Training to Help Traumatized Populations," United States Institute of Peace, Special Report 79, December 17, 2001. https: //www.usip.org/publications/2001/12/training -help-traumatized-populations.
19. Ibid.
20. Ibid.
21. Jennifer Freyd and Pamela Birrell, *Blind to Betrayal: When we fool ourselves we aren't being fooled* (Hoboken, NJ: Wiley Publishing, 2013).
22. Vamik Volkan, *Blind Trust: Large Groups and Their Leaders in Times of Crisis and Terror* (Charlottesville, VA: Pitchstone Publishing, 2004).

Chapter 4: Cycles of Violence from Unaddressed Trauma: STAR Model Part II

1. Richard Rohr, *Things hidden: Scripture as spirituality.* (Cincinnati, OH: Franciscan Media, 2008).
2. Diagnostic and Statistical Manual of Mental Disorders, Fifth Edition (Washington, DC: American Psychiatric Association, 2013).
3. ACE Study. ACE Response. Accessed February 2020. http://www.aceresponse.org/who_we_are/ACE-Study_43_pg.htm.
4. The enemy/aggressor cycle diagram and discussion are based on Enemy System Theory, Human Need Theory, and the writings of Olga Botchrova, Peter Levine, John E. Mack, Joseph Montville, Vamik Volkan, Walter Wink, and others.
5. Vamik Volkan, "Post Traumatic States: Beyond Individual PTSD in Societies Ravaged by Ethnic Conflict" in *Psychosocial Healing: A Guide for Practitioners*, eds. Paula Gutlove and Gordon Thompson (Cambridge, MA: Institute for Resource and Security Studies, 2003), 81.
6. Ibid., pp. 173–191.
7. Stephen Porges, "What is the Polyvagal Theory?" PsychAlive.org, published on April 23, 2018, YouTube video, 4:10, https://www.youtube.com/watch?v=ec3AUMDjtKQ.
8. Cabrera-Cruz, http://www.uni-klu.ac.at/~hstockha/neu/html/cabreracruz.htm.
9. John E. Mack, "Forward," in Vamik Volkan, *Cyprus: War and Adaptation: A Psychoanalytic History of Two Ethnic Groups in Conflict* (Charlottesville, VA: University of Virginia Press, 1979), ix-xxi.
10. Ibid., Volkan.

11. Pauline Boss, *Ambiguous Loss: Learning to Live with Unresolved Grief* (Cambridge, MA: Harvard University Press, 1999).
12. Olga Botcharova, "Implementation of Track Two Diplomacy," 293.
13. Walter Wink, *The Powers that Be: Theology for a New Millennium* (New York: Galilee, 1998), 91.
14. Lam Oryen Cosmas, "Breaking the Cycle of Violence," Mennonite Central Committee Peace Office Newsletter 34, no. 2, April-June 2004.
15. Gil Bailie, *Violence Unveiled: Humanity at the Crossroads* (New York: Crossroad, 1995).
16. *Forgiveness in Conflict Resolution: Reality and Utility, The Northern Ireland Experience*, Woodstock Theological Center Colloquium, Georgetown University, June 18, 1997, p. 54.
17. Vamik Volkan, *Blind Trust: Large Groups and Their Leaders in Times of Crisis and Terror* (Durham, NC: Pitchstone Publishing, 2004), 60–62.
18. Ibid.
19. Louise Diamond, Institute for Multi-Track Diplomacy, Arlington, VA. Accessed October 23, 2004. www .imtd.org.
20. Volkan, "Post-Traumatic States," in *Psychosocial Healing: A Guide for Practitioners,* 81.

Chapter 5: Breaking Cycles of Violence and Building Resilience: STAR Model Part III

1. Desmond Tutu in the introduction of *Forgiveness and Reconciliation,* eds. Raymond G. Helmick and Rodney L. Petersen (Radnor, PA: Templeton Foundation Press, 2001), xi.
2. Levine, *Waking the Tiger,* 193–194.
3. Cabrera-Cruz, http://www.uni-klu.ac.at/ ~ hstockha /neu/html/cabreracruz.htm.

4. *Psychosocial Healing: A Guide for Practitioners*, eds. Paula Gutlove and Gordon Thompson (Cambridge, MA: Institute for Resource and Security Studies, 2003).
5. Donna Minter, Minnesota Peacebuilding Leadership Institute, Minneapolis, MN, http://www .mnpeace.org/about.html.
6. Maria J. Stephan, "People Power Can Boost the Afghan Peace Process," *The Olive Branch* (blog), United States Institute of Peace, July 23, 2019, Accessed August 1, 2019, https://www.usip.org/blog /2019/07/people-power-can-boost-afghan-peace -process.
7. Erica Chenoweth and Maria J. Stephan, *Why Civil Resistance Works: The Strategic Logic of Nonviolent Conflict* (Columbia University Press, 2013), 30–82.
8. Erica Chenoweth and Maria J. Stephan, "How the World Is Proving Martin Luther King Right about Nonviolence," *The Washington Post*, January 18, 2016, Accessed August 1, 2019, https: //www.washingtonpost.com/news/monkey-cage /wp/2016/01/18/how-the-world-is-proving-mlk -right-about-nonviolence/?utm_term = .301 de1bc2781.
9. Chenoweth and Stephan, *Why Civil Resistance Works*, 202.
10. Maria J. Stephan, "Sojourners," Summit 2015 Talk, October 15, 2015. YouTube Video, 04:41, https: //www.youtube.com/watch?v = WkjWoXQlde0.
11. Maria J. Stephan, "People Power," https://www. usip.org/blog/2019/07/people-power-can-boost -afghan-peace-process?fbclid = IwAR3mS11h4Ha ZIbWPMV662oKQJzbk MPa8GwnyVuIGc11dHu 49qLVo7JBvXoE.

12. Chenoweth and Stephan, *Why Civil Resistance Works*, 11, 192–222.
13. Ibid.
14. Judith Lewis Herman in *Trauma and Recovery* uses the categories of safety, remembering and mourning, and reconnection. Paula Gutlove and Gordon Thompson use the categories of safety, acknowledgment, and reconnection. STAR uses breaking free/safety, acknowledgment, and reconnection in full-length trainings and breaking free/safety, truth, mercy, justice, peace/conflict transformation in shorter trainings.
15. See other *Little Book* titles for more information on the fields from which the trauma healing tools and processes are drawn: John Paul Lederach, *The Little Book of Conflict Transformation* (New York: Good Books, 2003); Lisa Schirch, *The Little Book of Strategic Peacebuilding* (New York: Good Books, 2004), and Howard Zehr, *The Little Book of Restorative Justice* (New York: Good Books, 2015).
16. A study in the former Yugoslavia demonstrated that providing a safe physical and psychological space for rebuilding old social contacts and meeting new people helped more than any other type of psychological intervention or therapy. From Gutlove and Thompson, 14.
17. Viktor Frankl, *Man's Search for Meaning* (New York: Pocket Books, 1997).
18. Mary B. Anderson and Marshall Wallace, *Opting Out of War: Strategies to Prevent Violent Conflict* (Boulder, CO: Lynne Rienner Publishers, 2013).
19. Botcharova, "Implementation of Track Two Diplomacy," 295–296.

20. Often the causes for which we would die are the same causes for which we are willing to kill. Here we speak of being willing to die *but not kill* for a cause.

21. Porges, *The Pocket Guide to the Polyvagal Theory*, 25.

22. Herbert Benson and Miriam Klipper, *The Relaxation Response* (New York: William Morrow Paperbacks; 2000).

23. Van der Kolk, *The Body Keeps the Score*.

24. Deb Dana, *The Polyvagal Theory in Therapy: Engaging the Rhythm of Regulation* (New York: W.W. Norton & Company, 2018).

25. Porges, *The Pocket Guide to the Polyvagal Theory*, 9, 25.

26. Ibid., 195.

27. Esther Harder, "Night Commuters and Soccer in Soroti," Mennonite Central Committee Peace Office Newsletter 34, no. 2: April-June 2004.

28. Betty Booker, "Blind Trust Author: Leader's Actions in Crisis Impel Conflict, Peace," Richmond Dispatch, Richmond, VA, October 4, 2004, Accessed October 5, 2004. See also Vamik Volkan, *Blind Trust: Large Groups and Their Leaders in Times of Crisis and Terror* (Charlottesville, VA: Pitchstone Publishing, 2004).

29. Botcharova, "Implementation of Track Two Diplomacy," 295–296.

30. Michael Lapsley, Unpublished Sermon, Cathedral of St. John the Divine, New York City, NY, May 5, 2002.

31. Resmaa Menaken, *My Grandmother's Hands: Racialized Trauma and the Pathway to Mending Our Hearts and Bodies* (Las Vegas, NV: Central Recovery Press, 2017).

32. Pat Ogden and Janina Fisher, *Sensorimotor Psychotherapy: Interventions for Trauma and Attachment* (New York: W. W. Norton & Company, 2015).

33. David Emerson and Elizabeth Hopper, PhD, *Overcoming Trauma through Yoga: Reclaiming Your Body* (Berkeley, CA: North Atlantic Books, 2011).

34. Peter Levine, *Waking the Tiger.*

35. Van der Kolk, *The Body Keeps the Score.*

36. Capacitar International provides many trauma release and self-regulation exercises, www.capacitar .org.

37. Gary Craig, "The Official Gary Craig EFT™ Training Centers," Official EFT™, www.emofree. com, or Dawson Church, "About EFT Tapping," EFT Universe, www.eftuniverse.com/faqs/about-eft -tapping-and-this-site.

38. Roger Callahan, "Professional Grade Energy Healing: Thought Field Therapy®," Callahan Techniques LTD, www.tfttapping.com.

39. David Berceli, "Tension and Trauma Release Exercises®", TRE® for All, Inc, www.traumaprevention .com.

40. Herman, *Trauma and Recovery,* 176.

41. Van der Kolk, *The Body Keeps the Score,* 203–208.

42. Pat Ogden and Janina Fisher, *Sensorimotor Psychotherapy.*

43. Neil Sattin, "How to Heal Your Trauma and Triggers with Peter Levine," Published by Relationship Alive on August 17, 2016, YouTube video, 44.53, https://www.youtube.com/watch?v = KUL8HU-SSs8.

44. Resmaa Menaken, *My Grandmother's Hands.*

45. Levine, *Waking the Tiger,* 188

46. "Eye Movement Desensitization and Reprocessing," EMDR Institute, Inc., www.emdr.com.

47. *Forgiveness in Conflict Resolution: Reality and Utility, The Bosnian Experience,* Woodstock Theological Center Colloquium, Georgetown University: October 24, 1997, 90.

48. Botcharova, "Implementation of Track Two Diplomacy," 299.

49. The film *For the Love of Tomorrow* tells the moving story of Irène Laure, a member of the French resistance in World War II, her struggle to acknowledge the destructiveness of her hatred when the war ended, and her eventual role in the reconciliation of Germany and France. *For the Love of Tomorrow,* produced by David Channer and Ian Corcoran (1985). DVD in seven languages at Initiatives of Change International, Streams at https://vimeo.com/157553174.

50. *Forgiveness in Conflict Resolution . . . The Bosnian Experience,* 82.

51. Botcharova, "Implementation of Track Two Diplomacy," 300.

52. Cabrera-Cruz, http://www.uni-klu.ac.at/~hstockha /neu/html/cabreracruz.htm.

53. For an individual and group example of transformative acknowledgment, see "Trauma, Connection, and Polarization" by Carolyn Yoder in David Brubaker et al., *When the Center Does Not Hold: Leadership in an Age of Polarization* (Minneapolis: Fortress Press, 2019).

54. It can be destabilizing for abuse survivors to meet with perpetrators or even family members to confront abuse if they are not supported. Restorative justice processes have been found to assist some survivors who request assistance in face-to-face or proxy meetings. RJ has stringent screening

guidelines, an extensive preparation protocol, and provides supportive accompaniment. See Judah Oudshoorn, Michelle Jackett, and Lorraine Stutzman, *The Little Book of Restorative Justice for Sexual Abuse: Hope through Trauma* (New York: Good Books, 2015).

55. Carolyn Yoder, phone conversation with Bessel A. van der Kolk, Trauma Center, Brookline, MA, February 23, 2005.

56. Patricia Mathes Cane, *Trauma Healing and Transformation: Awakening a New Heart with Body Mind Spirit Practices* (Watsonville, CA: Capacitar Inc., 2000).

57. Seeds of Peace, "Inspiring the Next Generation to Transform Conflict and Their Communities," New York, NY, http://www.seedsofpeace.org/mission.

58. Tom DeWolf and Jodie Geddes, *The Little Book of Racial Healing: Coming to the Table for Truth-Telling, Liberation, and Transformation* (New York, NY: Good Books, 2019).

59. September 11th Families for Peaceful Tomorrows, "Turning Grief into Actions for Peace," New York, NY, www.peacefultomorrows.org.

60. Fambul Tok International, www.fambultok. org. The first training of the reconciliation committee in the Fambul Tok process included much of the STAR curriculum, parts of which are still used in community trainings.

61. *Forgiveness in Conflict Resolution . . . The Northern Ireland Experience*, 54.

62. A suggested structure for such meetings is found in Gutlove and Thompson.

63. Bessel A. van der Kolk, "Traumatic Stress Disorder and the Nature of Trauma" in *Healing Trauma:*

Attachment, Mind, Body, and Brain, eds. Marion Solomon and Daniel Siegel (New York: W.W. Norton and Co., 2003), 188.

64. Stephen Porges, "What is the Polyvagal Theory?" https://www.youtube.com/watch?v=ec3AUMDjtKQ.

65. The "love hormone," oxytocin, is involved in our pleasure in reaching out to each other. Robert Malenka, MD, PhD, an oxytocin researcher, says, "With so much hatred and anger in the world, what could possibly be more important than understanding the mechanisms in the brain that make us want to be friendly with other people?"

66. Stanford University Medical Center, "Study shows how 'love hormone' oxytocin spurs sociability." Medical Press, September 28, 2017, https://medicalxpress.com/news/2017-09-hormone-oxytocin-spurs-sociability.html.

67. *Forgiveness in Conflict Resolution . . . The Northern Ireland Experience*, 69.

68. Levine, *Waking the Tiger,* 194.

69. Botcharova, "Implementation of Track Two Diplomacy," 92.

70. *Forgiveness in Conflict Resolution . . . The Northern Ireland Experience*, 5–6.

71. Hannah Arendt quoted in *Forgiveness in Conflict Resolution: Reality and Utility, The Northern Ireland Experience,* Woodstock Theological Center Colloquium, Georgetown University, June 18, 1997, 28.

72. *Forgiveness in Conflict Resolution . . . The Northern Ireland Experience*, 2.

73. Ibid., 83.

74. Susan Dominus and Pieter Hugo, "Portraits of Reconciliation," *New York Times Magazine,* April 6,

2014, http://www.nytimes.com/interactive/2014/04/06 /magazine/06-pieter-hugo-rwanda-portraits .html?_r = 0.

75. News and Press, Fambul Tok International, http: //www.fambultok.org/news-and-press.

76. Attributed to Bertolt Brecht. Quoted by Anthony Cary in *Forgiveness in Conflict Resolution: Reality and Utility, The Northern Ireland Experience,* Woodstock Theological Center Colloquium, Georgetown University, June 18, 1997, 28.

77. For more information, see Howard Zehr, *The Little Book of Restorative Justice* (New York: Good Books, 2002).

78. Sara Kershnar, Staci Haines, Gillian Harkins, et al. "Toward Transformative Justice: A Liberatory Approach to Child Sexual Abuse and Other Forms of Intimate and Community Violence," (generationFIVE, 2007), 1. www.transformative justice.eu/wp-content/uploads/2010/11/G5 _Toward_Transformative_Justice.pdf.

79. "Child Sexual Abuse Is a Social Justice Issue" gen-erationFIVE. www.generationfive.org/the-issue.

80. Robert Joseph, "Denial, Acknowledgement, and Peacebuilding through Reconciliatory Justice," Te Matahauariki Research Institute, August 2001, http://lianz.waikato.ac.nz/publications-working .htm.

81. Wilma Derksen lectures, trains, facilitates sup-port groups for homicide survivors, and organizes dialogues between victims and inmates in prison. www.wilmaderksen.com.

82. Turning Our Grief into Action for Peace, www .peacefultomorrows.org.

83. Torture Abolition and Survivors Support Coalition, Washington, DC, www.tassc.org.

84. *Forgiveness in Conflict Resolution . . . The Northern Ireland Experience*, 82.
85. Miroslov Volf, "Forgiveness, Reconciliation, and Justice," in *Forgiveness and Reconciliation*, eds. Raymond G. Helmick and Rodney L. Petersen (Radnor, PA: Templeton Foundation Press, 2001), 39.

Chapter 6: 9/11 and Breaking the Cycles, 2005 and 2019: Applying STAR

1. James O'Dea, *Cultivating Peace: Becoming a 21st Century Peace Ambassador* (Shift Books, 2012).
2. Jayne Seminare Docherty and Lisa Schirch, "A Long-Term Strategy for American Security," Center for Justice and Peacebuilding, Eastern Mennonite University. Written Fall 2001 in answer to the question, "So what would peacebuilders do about 9/11?" It contains short-term, intermediate (10 years), and long-term (50 years) strategies. https://emu.edu/now/news/2001/11/long-term-strategy-american-security.
3. For nine months, Mohandas Gandhi gave himself to "concerted meditation" to discern the next step in the Indian independence movement in 1930. The vision of the Salt March emerged from this period of prayer and meditation. From Ken Butigan, "Spiritual Practice in the Time of War," The Wolf: The Newsletter of Pace e Bene, Fall 2004, www.paceegne.org.
4. Neta C. Crawford, "United States Budgetary Costs of the Post-9/11 Wars Through FY2019: $5.9 Trillion Spent and Obligated," Watson Institute, Brown University, November 14, 2018, 3. https://watson.brown.edu/costsofwar/files/cow/imce

/papers/2018/Crawford_Costs%20of%20War%20
Estimates%20Through%20FY2019%20.pdf

5. Haley Britzky and Zachary Basu, "Global Terror
Attacks Have Skyrocketed Since 9/11," Axios
Newsletter, September 16, 2018, https://www
.axios.com/global-terror-attacks-have-skyrocketed
-since-911-34eec00f-ac8a-496f-8a30-
3f3f6d054110.html

6. "Why Afghanistan Is More Dangerous than
Ever," BBC News, September 14, 2018, https:
//www.bbc.com/news/world-asia-45507560.

7. Task Force on Extremism in Fragile States,
"Beyond the Homeland: Protecting America
from Extremism in Fragile States," United States
Institute of Peace, September 2018, https://www
.usip.org/sites/default/files/Taskforce-Extremism
-Fragile-States-Interim-Report.pdf.

8. Crawford, "United States Budgetary," 9.

9. Nikki Wentling, "VA Reveals Its Veteran Suicide
Statistic Included Active-Duty Troops" Stars and
Stripes, June 20, 2018, https://www.stripes.com
/news/us/va-reveals-its-veteran-suicide-statistic
-included active-duty-troops-1.533992.

Chapter 7: How Then Shall We Live?

1. Ervin Staub, *The Roots of Evil: The Origins of
Genocide and Other Group Violence* (Cambridge,
MA: Cambridge University Press, 1989).

2. Ibid., 20–21.

3. Joseph G. Bock, *Sharpening Conflict Management:
Religious Leadership and the Double-Edged Sword*
(Westport, CT: Praeger, 2001), 97.

4. Siegel, *Pocket Guide*, 27–1 to 27–3.

5. Chenoweth and Stephan, *Why Civil Resistance Works*, 6–7.
6. Gene Sharp, "198 Methods of Nonviolent Action," Albert Einstein Institution, https://www.aeinstein .org/nonviolentaction/198-methods-of-nonviolent -action.
7. Margaret J. Wheatley, *Who Do We Choose to Be? Facing Reality, Claiming Leadership, Restoring Sanity* (Oakland, CA: Berrett-Koehler Publishers, 2017), Prelude.

Selected Resources

Mary B. Anderson and Marshall Wallace, *Opting Out of War: Strategies to Prevent Violent Conflict* (Boulder, CO: Lynne Rienner Publishers, 2013).

Tom DeWolf and Jodie Geddes, *The Little Book of Racial Healing: Coming to the Table for Truth-Telling, Liberation, and Transformation* (New York: Skyhorse Publishing, 2019).

Peter A. Levine with Ann Frederick, *Waking the Tiger–Healing Trauma: The Innate Capacity to Transform Overwhelming Experiences* (Berkeley, CA: North Atlantic Books, 1997).

Resmaa Menaken, *My Grandmother's Hands: Racialized Trauma and the Pathway to Mending Our Hearts and Bodies* (Las Vegas, NV: Central Recovery Press, 2017).

Judah Oudshoorn, Michelle Jackett, and Lorraine Stutzman, *The Little Book of Restorative Justice for Sexual Abuse: Hope through Trauma* (New York, NY: Good Books, 2015).

Lisa Schirch, *The Ecology of Violent Extremism: Perspectives on Peacebuilding and Human Security*, Peace and Security in the 21st Century (Lanham, MD: Rowman & Littlefield International, 2018).

Bessel A. van der Kolk, *The Body Keeps the Score: Brain, Mind, and Body in the Health of Trauma* (New York: Viking Penguin Group, 2014), 347–356.

Viktor Frankl, *Man's Search for Meaning* (New York: Pocket Books, 1997).

Howard Zehr, *The Little Book of Restorative Justice* (Intercourse, PA: Good Books, 2015).

Nonviolence resources:
Peter Ackerman and Jack Duvall, *A Force More Powerful: A Century of Nonviolent Conflict* (New York: St. Martin's Press, 2001).

A Force More Powerful, Video series, available on Vimeo. Written and produced by Steve York, A production of York and Zimmerman Inc. and WETA, Washington, DC.

Teaching guides for *A Force More Powerful:*

- www.teachwithmovies.org/guides/force-more-powerful.html.
- www.peacelearner.org/2011/10/03/a-force-more-powerful/.

Nonviolence, Website geared to young people, www.nonviolence.com/why.

Resource Center for Nonviolence, www.rcnv.org.

Nonviolence International, www.nonviolenceinternational.net/wp/resources/resources.

International Center on Nonviolent Conflict, Online courses and resources in more than 70 languages and dialects, https://www.nonviolent-conflict.org.

About the Author

Carolyn E. Yoder is the Founding Director of STAR (Strategies for Trauma Awareness and Resilience), a training program of the Center for Justice and Peacebuilding at Eastern Mennonite University in Virginia. She worked as an educator and psychotherapist in Asia, East and Southern Africa, the Middle East, and the Caucuses for more than 18 years. She has a private psychotherapy practice specializing in transforming trauma and offers online resources at www.PeaceAfterTrauma.com. She holds an MA in Counseling Psychology from Alliant International University and an MA in Linguistics from the University of Pittsburgh. She and her husband, Rick, live in Harrisonburg, VA. They have three daughters and four grandchildren.

The Little Book of Trauma Healing, Revised and Updated
ORDER FORM

If you would like to order multiple copies of *The Little Book of Trauma Healing, Revised and Updated* for groups you know or are a part of, please email **bookorders@skyhorsepublishing.com** or fax order to **(212) 643-6819**. (Discounts apply only for more than one copy.)

Photocopy this page and the next as often as you like.

The following discounts apply:

1 copy	$5.99
2-5 copies	$5.39 each (a 10% discount)
6-10 copies	$5.09 each (a 15% discount)
11-20 copies	$4.79 each (a 20% discount)
21-99 copies	$4.19 each (a 30% discount)
100 or more	$3.59 each (a 40% discount)

Free Shipping for orders of 100 or more!

Prices subject to change.

Quantity　　　　　　　　　　　　*Price*　　　　*Total*

_____ copies of　*The Little Book of Trauma Healing @*　_____　_____

(Standard ground shipping costs will be added for orders of less than 100 copies.)

METHOD OF PAYMENT

❐   Check or Money Order
      *(payable to **Skyhorse Publishing** in U.S. funds)*

❐   Please charge my:
❐ MasterCard ❐ Visa
❐ Discover   ❐ American Express
_____

Exp. date and sec. code_____

Signature _____

Name _____

Address _____

City_____

State _____

Zip_____

Phone_____

Email _____

SHIP TO: (if different)
Name _____

Address _____

City_____

State _____

Zip_____

Call: (212) 643-6816
Fax: (212) 643-6819
Email: bookorders@skyhorsepublishing.com
(do not email credit card info)